The Almost Complete Collection Of

True Singapore Ghost Stories

BOOK 10

Russell Lee
& team of ghost writers

Angsana Books

Published by  Angsana Books

Angsana Books is an imprint of

FLAME OF THE FOREST PUBLISHING Pte Ltd
Blk 5 Ang Mo Kio Industrial Park 2A
#07-22/23, AMK Tech II, Singapore 567760
Tel: (65) 6484 8887, Fax: (65) 6484 2208
mail@flameoftheforest.com

www.flameoftheforest.com

Printed in Singapore

ISBN 978-981-3056-18-3

Say your prayers little one
Don't forget, my son
To include everyone
Tuck you in, warm within
Keep you free from sin
Till the Sandman he comes
    Sleep with one eye open
    Gripping your pillow tight

—*Enter Sandman*
by Metallica

AUTHOR'S NOTE

It's been 10 years since True Singapore Ghost Stories (Book 1) was published. When I started back then, uppermost in my mind was entertaining readers. Now, after a decade of compiling stories and receiving thousands of letters, much feedback and nine other books in the series, entertainment is still my top priority. I know my readers much better too. Which is why I'd like to thank you for your support and friendship. Your positive comments spur me on to do my best in each book.

Meanwhile, my team of "ghost writers" is always changing. You know how ghosts are; they can get out of control and that's when I have to exorcise them from the team. Author Damien Sin remains the most prolific contributor. The irrepressible Sin is a well of ideas and has an unorthodox, immensely readable style.

Frankie Fearless is also a regular although I often wonder why a person afraid of the dark uses the name "Fearless". Top journalist Ida Bachtiar has been a member of team since the very first Book 1. And the latest recruit is James Lee, author of the Mr Midnight series. What all team members have in common is the ability to tell a good story.

Besides entertainment, the stories also reflect reality: good eventually triumphs over evil and a day of reckoning is sure for the bad. I never ever encourage occult practices but I do think that spirits and ghosts exist. I feel that they cannot harm the living unless you invite trouble.

And do remember that I only write for Angsana's True Singapore Ghost Stories. It's easy to tell the genuine series: first, check to make sure you can see the Angsana mark, and, second, check if the series has the one and only True Singapore Ghost Stories Book 1. If these two marks are there, then you have the genuine stuff in your hands. If not, don't buy the book!

Good press still thrills us no end. One review that caught my eye recently was carried in the "Visitor's Guide to Singapore". It said that Angsana's True Singapore Ghost Stories series was "uniquely Singaporean"!

The "Visitor's Guide to Singapore" gives the thumbs-up to Angsana's True Singapore Ghost Stories series.

Even after 10 books, the question is still asked: Are the stories true? I take those who send in their stories at their word. Anyway, you ought to read this book for enjoyment, not to do research. Some stories are obviously tongue-in-cheek and so you have to read it in the right "spirit". Some stories may seem unreal but there's a moral and a "feel good" effect at the end.

Each book is crafted so that you'll experience a range of emotions. Not all stories are meant to be bloodcurdling. Wit and subtlety are key ingredients. There's also poignancy; sometimes you might just go away with a strange, uneasy feeling. More than anything else, I hope you'll have a good time, even if you have a few scares along the way!

Before I end, I'd like to mention an article in "Singapore Book World" by Dr Kirpal Singh, an English literature professor. It was an insightful article and I agree with its contents. Dr Kirpal reported that most Singaporeans were quite familiar with Russell Lee's stories. Which leads me to another question often asked: Why are the books so popular? To be honest, there's no clear answer but I put it down to good storytelling.

It shouldn't surprise us that there are some Singaporeans who, like Dr Kirpal writes, "cringe" at what most of us like to read. And they think that everybody else should be as they are and read what they read! Alamak, sudah-lah. Bo chap! I do enjoy teh sarabat and roti prata, char kway teow and kopi-o, or nasi lemak, even though it may not be Mr Rich Snob Singaporean's cup of tea.

For too long, we've been led to believe the excuse that the reason for poor book sales by Singapore authors is that "good art doesn't sell". That's a cop out! Look closely and you'll notice that most times these books don't sell because they're "bad art", the kind of work that Mr Snob indulges in. Consider this: How can people who lead empty, boring lives write anything substantial? Like the innocent little boy who saw clearly and cried that the emperor was stark naked, we, the majority folk, must not hesitate to call a spade a spade.

Be true to yourself, be cool. Chase away the demons that oppress your mind.

One more thing: we are offering $500 for mint copies of the original True Singapore Ghost Stories Book 1. They've become a rarity and we are trying to get hold of a few copies ourselves. Despite numerous appeals, it seems that those who do have the book are not willing to part with it. I hope $500 is enough to tempt you. But they must be mint copies and we reserve our right to decide what's "mint".

The Almost Complete Collection of

TRUE Singapore GHOST STORIES

By **RUSSELL LEE** and a team of ghost writers

The original Book 1, worth at least $500.

And now that I've finished Book 10, I'm preparing for the next 10 books! But don't you worry about that. Just enjoy the book that's in your hands right now. As the Metallica song goes:

> *Exit: Light*
> *Enter: Night*
> *Take my hand*
> *We're off to never never land.*

russelllee@flameoftheforest.com

Dear Readers,

What I like most about your letters is the enthusiasm you show. This is apparent in the letters that have been selected for print on "The Front Page" and "The Back Page". Please excuse me for not being able to reply to each letter. Some of you are quite regular and I'm beginning to get to know you quite well.

I'd like to bid a special welcome to the readers from East Malaysia, especially those from Miri, Kota Kinabalu, Kuching and Sibu. Join in the fun!

I've decided to increase the cash prize in the next book to $2,000. This means that there will be even more cash winners.

For the Book 9 Angsana Russell Lee Writers' Contest, the prizes awarded include software from Microsoft, cassette radios from Sanyo Malaysia Sdn Bhd and leather diaries from Grandluxe Pte Ltd.

The cash winners of the Book 9 contest are listed below.

The $500 winner is:

TAN LITING

The $100 winners are:

DELWYN LEE
  35, Jln Permas, Johor Baru
CHEN PEIYU
  Blk 770, Choa Chu Kang St 54

MUHAMMAD HAFIZ BIN MD SALLEH

ADEQ
  Blk 730 Woodlands Circle

ONG ANN HUAT
  Blk 603 Ang Mo Kio Ave 5
JASMINE CHEW
  Blk 936, Jurong West St 91

And thanks for your letters:

ABDRAJAK SALIM
  P.O. Box 34, 91207, Kunak, Sabah
ABDUL FAIZALBIN ABDUL HALIM
  Blk 336 Bt Batok St 32
ADELENE LOH WEN LI
  Blk 27 Lor Lew Lian
ADELINE LEE

  Blk 28 Jln Bt Merah
ADELINE LEE YI QING
  Sennett Pl
ADELINE PENG
  Blk 319 Ang Mo Kio Ave 1
ADEQ
  Blk 730 Woodlands Circle

AGNES BAY LEE TENG
  Blk 20 Toa Payoh Lor 7
AGNES LAU MEI LIN
  Blk 524 Serangoon North Ave 4
AHMAD FATHI BIN MANSOR
  Blk 702 Woodlands Dr 40
ALAN CHIAM YONG MENG

Blk 547 Ang Mo Kio Ave 10
ALAN VAZ
Jln Puyu, Tmn Bonong, 83000, B. Pahat, Johor
ALAN YEO CHOON PHENG
Blk 874 Tampines St 82
ALBERT TEO GUI XIONG
Blk 707 Yishun Ave 5
ALEX ANG
Blk 44 Bedok South Rd
ALFERA SVRIANTI BTE SABTU
Blk 657 Woodlands Ring Rd
ALFRED WONG
Blk 704 Hougang Ave 2
ALICE HO KIT SAN
Blk 130 Bedok North St 2
ALICIA YANG QUANZHEN
Blk 116 Simei St 1
ALLAN PHUA JOON YEN
Blk 117 Yishun Ring Rd
AMIRAH FATIN BTE MOHAMMED SAFIEE
Blk 427 Tampines St 41
AMOL ANANT PARAB
Blk 301 Bt Batok St 31
AMY KOH MIAO CI
Blk 93 Whampoa Dr
ANDREA LEONG WEN HSI
Bloxhome Dr
ANDREW JOSEPH
Loyang Rise
ANDRIEANNA QUAH SU ANN
Jln SS2/18 SEA Park 47300. Petaling Jaya, Selangor
ANDY COLE
Blk 1 St George's Rd
ANDY GN SWEE KENG
Blk 619 Hougang Ave 8
ANDY TAY BOON CHEW
Blk 701 Hougang Ave 2
ANDY YAN KAI CONG
Blk 173 Bt Batok West Ave 8
ANG SHI JUN
Blk 559 Ang Mo Kio Ave 10
ANG XIAO HUI
Blk 804 King George's Ave
ANGEL LI'L
Jln Tanjung 5/4, 46000 P Jaya, Selangor
ANGEL TAN HSIANG CHIN
Blk 863 Tampines St 83
ANGELA QUEK HUI YING
Blk 611 Ang Mo Kio Ave 5
ANGELINE KHOO YING LI
Blk 323 Jurong East St 31
ANGELINE TEOH LENG SIM
Blk 418 Woodlands St 41
ANGIE CHEAH YONG LING
1st floor, Jln Lim Swee Sim, 86000, Kluang, Johor
ANN KSH
Blk 604 Clementi West St 1
ANN-MAREE
ANNE A. M. LIM
Blk 209 Yishun St 21
ANTONIUS WIDJAJA
Blk 151A King's Rd
ARYANY
ASHLEY GAY
Blk 271 Choa Chu Kang Ave 2
AZHAR BIN AHMAD
Blk 41 Bedok South Rd
BALJINAER SINGH
Persiaran Pegoh Aman 4, Taman Desa Aman, 31500 Lahat, Perak
BAVANI
BELINDA GWEE KEJIA
Blk 786 Yishun Ring Rd
BENMIN CHAI HO CHIN
Blk 395 Tampines Ave 7
BILL HENG HAN
BINDHU
BJORN TAN JIA WEI
Blk 629 Bedok Reservoir Rd

BRENDAN CHEW
Blk 326 Ang Mo Kio Ave 3
BRENDON TAY BINGLUN
Blk 375 Clementi Ave 4
C HOH
Blk 301 Tampines St 32
CALVIN LEE CHEONG WEI
Blk 406 Fajar Rd
CALVIN TAY KAI BOON
Blk 339 Woodlands Ave 1
CANCER
Blk 731 Tampines St 71
CHAI C. S.
Blk 6 Marine Ter
CHAMMON NG CHEI YON
Blk 554 Chua Chu Kang North 6
CHAN HARIZ
Blk 164 Jln Teck Whye
CHAN SIEW YIN
Blk 266 Yishun St 22
CHAN XIANG RONG
Blk 537 Jurong West Ave 1
CHAN YING HUAN
Blk 651 Hougang Ave 8
CHANG NGEE KHIONG
Jln Sungai Tengah, Matang, 93050 Kuching, Sarawak
CHEN LICHI
Blk 345 Batok West Ave 5 St 34
CHEN MEI XIU
Blk 413 Pandan Gdn
CHEN PEIYU
Blk 770 Choa Chu Kang St 54
CHEN XIAO QI
Blk 906
CHEN YI
Blk 119 Yishun Ring Rd
CHEN YONG KAI
Blk 553 Ang Mo Kio Ave 10
CHERYL MARIANNE WOO XUE ER
Jln Tari Payong
CHEW KIA HONG
Blk 171 Bedok South Rd
CHIA KAIPENG
Blk 916 Tampines St 91
CHITRA SHANMUGHAM
Jln Datu Yusuf Shahbudin 15 Taman Sentosa Klang 41200
CHNG HUI ZI
Blk 44 Bendemeer Rd
CHNG YEOH BENG
Green Rd One, 11600, Penang
CHONG YING YING
Blk 619 Hougang Ave 8
CHRISTAL
CHRISTINA TANG PUI TENG
Blk 178 Ang Mo Kio Ave 4
CHRISTOPHER YAK BING SHENG
Blk 331 Jurong East Ave 1
CHUA ENG HOU
Blk 321 Hougang Ave 5
CHUA HERN CHIH
Blk 8 Teban Gdn
CHUA KENT TART
Tabuan Dusun, Lor Kedandi No. 6, 93350 Kuching, Sarawak
CHUA WEN JUN
Blk 514 Bt Batok St 52
CLARENCE CHUA
Chestnut Lane, Upp Bt Timah Rd
CLARICE CHNG YUAN WEN
Blk 112 Bedok Reservoir Rd
CLAUDIA
CLEMENT HUANG
COLIN LIM TZE PING
Seletar Rd
CRYSTAL NG
Blk 554 Choa Chu Kang North 6
CYNTHIA YANG TING TING
Blk 263 Yishun St 22
D CHANG
Jln Chew Peng Loon, Ipoh Gdn, 31400,

Perak
D. KOTNARY
DAMANSARA
Jaya Tamar St, Ringwood, 3134 Victoria
DAMIEN LAU ZHE HONG
Blk 205 Bishan St 23
DAN PHUA HONG HAO
Blk 696 Hougang St 61
DANIEL LIM SAY LIANG
Blk 108 Jln Rajah
DANIEL POON JUN WEN
Blk 221 Yishun St 21
DANIEL TAN
Blk 415 Hougang Ave 10
DARRYL YIN ZIAN GUO
Blk 35 Chai Chee Ave
DATIN SURAIDAH P. TIU
DAVID CHUA
DEBORAH LOH
P.O.Box 1270, Gadong 3112, BSB BE3978, Brunei
DELWYN LEE
Jln Permas 1/27, Tmn Permas Jaya, 81750 Masai, Johor Baru
DERRICK YAP DELI
Blk 324 Tah Ching Rd
DESMOND CHIA HAN CHIN
Blk 4 Syed Alwi Rd
DIANA YAO JIE XIN
Rambai Rd
DIANA YEO SIEW CHING
Blk 237 Hougang St 21
DIN BIN ABDUL RAHMAN
Blk 3 Hougang Ave 3
DINAH BT HJ SERUDIN
279 Kg Lambak Kiri, Jln Berakas, BB1314, Brunei Darussalam
DONG MEIYI
Blk 18 Bedok South Rd
DOROTHY POH SIU ING
Walmer Dr
EDWARD LIM JUM WEI
Blk 501 Jurong West St 51
EDWINA KOH HUI NA
Blk 105 Woodlands St 13
EEU PETER
Blk 128 Bt Merah View
EILEEN CHAN
ELAIN KOK
Blk 109 Teck Whye L
ELRIC HENG
Blk 66 Commonwealth Dr
ELSIE NG
Blk 116 Ang Mo Kio Ave 4
ERIC CHAN YING HAO
Blk 121 Bedok Reservoir Rd
ERIC TAN
20 Irrawaddy Rd
ESTHER FONG VIE NIE
Jln Kampung Pisang, 11500 Ayer Itam, Penang
EUGENE
Taiping, Perak
EUGENE LIANG
Blk 141 Jln Bt Merah
EVELYN TAN (EVA)
Jln Lancang 2, Tmn Bkt Sri Cheras, 56100, KL
EVON NG BEE HWA
Blk 410 Woodlands St 41
EVONNE ONG SHER TING
FAZREEN BIN IRHAMMUDDIN
Blk 327 Tan Ching Rd
FOO MING FENG
35 Jurong East Ave 1
FRANK WOON
Jln Murni 3, Taman Murni, 83000, Batu Pahat, Johor
GABRIEL LALITHA
Blk 222 Yishun St 21
GABRIEL LEE SWEE KEAT
Poole Rd

GAN WEI XUAN
  Blk 319 Bt Batok West Ave 4
GARY PHUA MENG HONG
  Blk 536 Hougang St 52
GARY TAN YUAN JUN
  Blk 222 Bt Batok Ave 3
GARY WOON CHONG SHENG
  Blk 491D Tampines St 45
GERMAINE MERCEDES HENDRIN
  Blk 455 Sin Ming Ave
GERRARD LAI CHANGMIN
  Blk 18 Hougang Ave 8
GOH CHEE KIONG
  Blk 114 Potong Pasir Ave 1
GOH CHING YAW
  Blk 240 Yishun Ring Rd
GOH MEI HUA
  Blk 5 Telok Blangah Cres
GRACE GOH EAN CHEE
  Jln 2, Taman Sri Ukay, 68000, Ulu Klang,
  KL
GRACE NG YEE LING
  Neram Rd
GRACE TAN
  Pemimpin Dr, Marymount View
HAIQAL HAJA MAIDEN
  Blk 640 Choa Chu Kang St 64
HAN QIUYUE
  Blk 1 Delta Ave
HARON BIN RAHMAT
  Blk 150 Bedok Reservoir Rd
HATIEZA SYAIFA
  Tmn Peong, Lor 6A9 Matang Jaya,
  93050, Kuching, Sarawak
HEMA HISHAM BIN KAMSANI
  Blk 337 Jurong East St 32
HO CHIN SWEE
  Blk 733 Yishun Ave 5
HO HWEE CHUAN
  Blk 214 Tampines St 23
HO SI HUI
HO YEOW MIN
  Blk 104B Ang Mo Kio St 11
HOH YEE HUN
  Blk 213 Ang Mo Kio Ave 3
HTOO ZAW
  Blk 428 Woodlands St 41
HUANG HAOTENG
  Blk 170 Bt Batok West Ave 8
HUANG SHIFEI
  Blk 317 Jurong East St 31
HUANG ZUDA
  Blk 323 Serangoon Ave 3
HUNG HING YAU
  Blk 811 Jurong West St 81
IAN KHOO ENG HONG
  Jln Mas Puteh
IRENE ONG AI LING
  Blk 5 Upp Aljunied Lane
ISKANDAR DZULGARNAIN BIN
MOHAMMAD
  Blk 178 Woodlands St 13
IVAN CHEW HUAN JIE
  Blk 136 Serangoon North Ave 2
IVY CHAI
  Jln Foochow, Lor JB, 93300, Kuching,
  Sarawak
JACKIE FOO YIT SHIN
  Lorong Waton(1), Taman Sri Wat, 68000
  Ampang, Selangor
JACQUELINE CHOO CHIA MING
  Blk 54 Geylang Bahru
JAMIE CHANG SU LIN
  Lor Chateau, Taman Chateau 30250
  Ipoh, Perak
JAMILAH BTE IDRIS
  Blk 464 Jurong West St 41
JAMINE TAN
  Upp Paya Lebar Rd
JASMINE CHEW XUE FEN
  Blk 936 Jurong West St 91
JASMINE TAN YING YIN
  Upp Paya Lebar Rd

JASON LAI
  Blk 139 Jln Bt Merah
JASON POH
  Blk 43 Jurong East Ave 1
JASON TEO KENG HOCK
  Blk 276 Yishun St 22
JEFFREY CHAN
  Blk 322 Bt Batok St 33
JENNY TAY GOON GUEK
  Blk 2 Bedok South Ave 1
JEREMY CHUA JIAKAI
  Blk 794 Yishun Ring Rd
JESLIN NEO JIE LIN
  Blk 115 Pending Rd
JESS SOH M.L.
  Blk 481 Jurong West St 41
JESSIE NG WAN QING
  Blk 458 Jurong West St 41
JEY KISHAN
  Jln Teratai 31, Tmn Johor Jaya, 81100
  Johor
JIANZHI
JILL YONG
JOANNE CHNG
  Blk 106 Jln Bt Merah
JONATHAN
  Blk 501 Bedok North St 3
JONE
  Blk 661 Yishun Ave 4
JOSEPH
JOSEPH KWA
  Blk 513 Ang Mo Kio St 53
JOSEPHINE
JOSHUA NEOH WENG FEI
  Gerbang Erskine, Penang
JOYCE LEE MEI LI
  Blk 42 Beo Cres
JR
JUDD YEOW
  Blk 45 Bedok South Rd
JUDITH
  Jln Kelinai 2, Jln Pujut 7, 98000 Miri,
  Sarawak
JUITA BTE ZUKIMAN
  Blk 274 Yishun St 22
JULIA LIM BEE YAN
  Blk 306 Bt Batok St 31
JULIAN CHEN QI YUAN
  Blk 224 Pending Rd
JULIET LEE
JUREEN CHEN ZHEN ZHI
  Blk 351 Ubi Ave 1
JUSTIN YEO SOON HENG
K. HARIGARAN
  Blk 191 Bishan St 13
KARTHIK
  Blk 334 Hougang Ave 5
KATHY NG KAI SHI
  Blk 227 Bt Panjang Pending Rd
KAVITHA
  Blk 139 Potong Pasir Ave 3
KEALVIN LEE
  Jln Perlak 3, Sri Petaling, Paskode
  57000, Kuala Lumpur
KEITH YONG MUN
KEN NEO GUAN HENG
  Blk 504 Choa Chu Kang St 51
KEVIN JOHN
  Blk 1 Short St
KHAIRIL SHAH
  Blk 158 Toa Payoh Lor 1
KHO GEOK KHIM
  Blk 131 Cashew Rd
KIRANJIT KAUR SIDHU
  Jln Mersing 86000 Kluang, Johor
KISHAN KUMAR SINGH
  Blk 234 Simei St 4
KOH RENBIN
  Blk 151 Toa Payoh Lor 2
KOH TAT KIAN
  Tanjung Kling, Kampung Hailam, 76400,
  Malacca

KUA EE WEN
  Jln SS19/1, 47500, Subang Jaya, PJ,
  Selangor
KUMARAN S/O BALASUBRAMANIAM
  Blk 322 Jurong East St 31
LAWRENCE CHANG JIE QIANG
  Blk 625 Bt Batok Central
LAZARUS PAO
  Custom Flat, Jln Lawan Danut 98850
  Lawas,Sarawak
LE RAINE ELEANOR HENDRIK
  Blk 455 Sin Ming Ave
LEE BOON PIAN
  Blk 557 Jurong West St 42
LEE KIT MUN
  Blk 42 Beo Cres
LEE SI HUI
  Blk 902 Tampines Ave 4
LEE WEE SIAN
  Blk 263 Tampines St 21
LEMON WONG
  Blk 653 Yishun Ave 4
LENG SUN
  Blk 535 Ang Mo Kio Ave 5
LEONARD ANG JUN WEI
  Blk 116 Ang Mo Kio Ave 4
LEOW KAR GEA
  Blk 670 Hougang Ave 8
LEOW SHI LING
  Blk 5 Hillview Ave
LESLIE LIM
  Miri, Sarawak
LESLIE TAN JIEKAI
  Blk 156 Yung Loh Rd
LESTER CHIA WEIXIAN
  Ee Teow Leng Rd
LIANA
  Ang Mo Kio
LILIAN ONG LAY LIAN
  Blk 5 Jln Minyak
LILY LOH LEI HENG
  Blk 128 Kim Tian Rd
LIM CHU FENG
  Blk 39 Jln Rumah Tinggi
LIM KAH YING
  Blk 245 Tampines St 21
LIM KOK KIONG
  Blk 228 Bukit Batok Central
LIM MICHAEL
  Blk 917 Jurong West St 91
LIM QUN BAO
  Blk 726 Woodlands Circle
LIM SIEW MEI
LIM WEE HEONG
  Blk 268 Yishun St 22
LIM YEE SHUEN
  Blk 129 Kim Tian Rd
LIM YI WEN
  Blk 405 Choa Chu Kang Ave 3
LIN JING HONG
  Blk 7 Haig Rd
LINDA MOURIN D/O MICHEL
TENNAMARAM
  Palm Oil Mill, 45600 Berjuntai, Selangor
  D.E.
LINDAWATI
  Amber Rd, Parkway Mansion
LING HUA PIN
  Jln Keranji, Taman Melodies, 80250,
  Johor Bahru
LIONEL NG
  Blk 407 Chua Chu Kang Ave 3
LIU JIAN RONG
  Blk 165 Yishun Ring Rd
LIUS WIDJAJA
  Blk 151A King's Rd
LOH KE XIN
  Jln Nevena Uarta
LOH HAN HONG
  Jln Bentara Dalam, Tmn Iskandar, 80500,
  Johor Bahru
LOH SOH TING
  Blk 410 Saujana Rd

LOW CHER HEANG
Blk 450G Tampines St 42
M. SALIHIN BIN ROSLI
Blk 808 Woodlands St 81
MANDY NG HUIYI
Blk 208 Yishun St 21
MARCUS TAN
Blk 132 Geylang East Ave 1
MARIA ROBERTSON AND KELLY
MALINA
MATHAN
Blk 720 Yishun St 11
MATHAN
Blk 720 Yishun St 71
MAVDEENAH BTEM ABDUL GUANI
Blk 223 Pasir Ris St 21
MD FEROZ S/O MYA AYE
Blk 737 Yishun St 72
MD SHAHRIZAL BIN HOSEN
Blk 62 Commonwealth Dr
MD ZHARIF KHAN
Blk B11 Changi Village Rd #17
MELISSA CHAN
Ipoh
MELVIN DONG HANWEN
Blk 826 Yishun St 81
MERILYN LEE WANCHIA
MICHELLE CHIANG HUILING
Blk 522 Serangoon North Ave 4
MICHELLE HO
Blk 841 Woodlands St 82
MOHAMED AMIN
Blk 83 Redhill Lane
MOHAMMAD FARHAT
Blk 20 Chai Chee Rd
MOHAMMAD NASER BIN AHMAD
Blk 208 Boon Lay Pl
MOHAMMAD ZAKI BIN ZAKARIA
Blk 229 Pending Rd
MOHD SHAHNAZ
Jln Taman Pantai, 59100 Kuala Lumpur
MOHD SHARWANI
Blk 527 Jurong West St 52
MOHD ABDUL KADIR BIN ABDUL SALAM
Blk 239 Bt Batok East Ave 5
MOHD ALIF RIDWAN
Blk 44 Bendemeer Rd
MOHD RIZAL BIN ABD RASHID
Blk 99 Bedok North Ave 4
MOK TSE LING
Tampines St 41
MUGUNTHAN S/O RAMASAMY
Blk 616 Hougang Ave 8
MUHAIMIN BIN HAMADI
Blk 661 Yishun Ave 4
MUHAMMAD FAIZAL BIN MOHMAD
Blk 450 Jurong West St 42
MUHAMMAD SAMER
Blk 518 West Coast Rd
MUHAMMAD AJIB BIN HJ AHMAD AURAL
Flat Anggrek Desa Berakas 3786 Brunei
Darussalam
MUHAMMAD AZREE BIN ABDUL RAHIM
Blk 312 Bt Batok St 32
MUHAMMAD HAFIZ BIN MD. SALLEH
MUHAMMAD KHAIRUL BIN ISHAK
Blk 353 Yishun Ring Rd
MUHD SIRAJ
Blk 108 Bedok Reservoir Rd
MUHD HAFIZ BIN ISHAK MAGNUS
Blk 112 Bedok Reservoir Rd
MUHD HIDAYAT BIN ISNIN
Blk 727 Jurong West Ave 5
MUHD KHAIRUL BIN RALS
Blk 264 Bishan St 24
MUHDAZAHARBIN ROSHI
Blk 776 Yishun Ave 2
MUI SZE LING
Spg 705, Kg Jangsak, Jln Gadong 3190,
BSB, Brunei Darussalam
MUSTAQIM BIN HASNI
Blk 402 Hougang Ave 10

NADIAH BTE ANUAR
Blk 214 Tampines St 23
NANNARDIAN BTE MOHD TAHIR
Blk 142 Bedok Reservoir Rd
NASRIN
Blk 17 Teban Gdns
NATALIE
Blk 892 Tampines Ave 8
NEO CHI LIN
NEO KAI LING
Blk 285 Yishun Ave 6
NEOH ENG SUAN
Klinik Edsihatan Simpang Empat, 06650
Alor Setar, Kedah, Malaysia
NG JIAYING
NG JING WEN
NG MEIFANG
Blk 154 Jln Teck Whye
NG XIAO XIAO
Blk 409 Tampines St 41
NG YIWEN
Blk 518 West Coast Rd
NGO HEA MENG
NIAN WEE CHERN
Blk 170 Bt Batok West Ave 8
NICHOLAS MAH SENG KONG
Jln Delima 13, Taman Bk Melaka, Bt
Beruang 75450, Malacca
NINA KAVA
Blk 16 Upp Boon Keng Rd
NOR ALFIAN BIN NOR ANUAR
Blk 111 Woodlands St 13
NORADIZANA
NORIMAH BTE BACHIK
Blk 381 Clementi Ave 5
NUR LIYANA KHAIRUDDIN
Blk 165 Simei Rd
NUR AISHAH BTE MD. UNOS
Blk 246 Kim Keat Link
NUR AZIZAH BTE KAMARUDIN
Blk 25 Eunos Cres
NUR SRI DEWI BTE RAHMAT
Blk 41 Tanglin Halt Rd
NURALISIA MD SAINI
Blk 17 Teban Gdn
NURSHAFAWATI BTE MOHD YUSOF
Blk 467 Jurong West St 41
NURTASHA BTE JA'AFAR
Blk 436 Jurong West Ave 1
NURUL JANNAH BTE HAMZAH
Blk 540 Serangoon North Ave 4
NUURFAZANAH BTE ABDUL SALAM
Blk 144 Tampines St 12
OH SEOK YUN
Blk 132 Jln Bt Merah
ONG ANN AIK
Blk 603 Ang Mo Kio Ave 5
ONG ANN HUAT
Blk 603 Ang Mo Kio Ave 5
ONG BING SHAO
Blk 275 Bangkit Rd
ONG MING CHONG
Blk 116 Jurong East St 13
ONG Y. H.
Blk 25 Chai Chee Rd
P. SARAVANAN
Blk 160 Woodlands St 13
P. W. YOON
Regat Hock Lee, Ipoh Gdn, 31400 Ipoh,
Perak
PALLISTER LOH JIE XIANG
Jln Midah Barat, Tmn Midah, 56000
Kuala Lumpur
PAMELA KOH
Blk 291 Bishan St 24
PAMELA TAN
Blk 792 Woodlands Ave 6
PANVSELVAM S/O SICKALINGAM
Blk 688 Jurong West Central 1
PATRICIA LOO YIN YIN
Lintang Macallum 2. 10300 Penang
PEARLIN POH

Blk 334 Ubi Ave 1
PEH LIN YEE
Blk 10 Joo Seng Rd
PHOEBE LEE SU WEN
10 Flora Rd
PHOON YONG KONG
Blk 454 Jurong West St 42
PHYSILIA
RAGU S/O THERENTHRAN
Blk 194 Kim Keat Ave
RAJU
RANDIE TAN
Blk 723 Yishun St 71
RAYNER TAN KAY JIN
Blk 2 Marine Vista
RAYNER WONG
Blk 94C Bedok North Ave 4
RENA LEE CHING HUI
Blk 115 Teck Whye Lane
RENEE YONG
RICHARD METCALFE
Rushmere Dr, Sault Ste. Marie, ON
Canada P6C 2T3
RODRIGUES BASIL FRANCIS
Blk 22 Havelock Rd
RONALD BOLI STELZER
Blk 430 Tampines St 41
RONALD CHUA ZHI HONG
Blk 729 Jurong West St 72
RONALD WENG
Blk 315 Ubi Ave 1
RONNIE AHMAD
Spg 38 Perpindahan Lambak Kanan,
3695, Brunei Darussalam
ROSELIN LOO MEOW JUAN
Blk 627 Bedok Reservoir Rd
S. KARTHIGEYAN
Blk 621 Ang Mo Kio Ave 9
SAFIAH SULAIMAN
Blk 864 Tampines St 83
SAHLIZA HAZURA BTE HARUN
Jln Rengam, Simpang Rengam, 86200,
Kluang, Johor
SAIDILROSLAN BIN RAHMAD
Blk 255 Tampines St 21
SALLY TAN
Elliot Rd
SAMANTHA SOH
Blk 232 Hougang Ave 1
SAMUEL GOH WEI QIANG
Blk 1 Ghim Moh Rd
SANGEETHA D/O PRAGASAM
Blk 866 Woodlands St 83
SARJUNE IBRAHIM
Blk 112 Depot Rd
SAUL ANG WEE WOON
Blk 842H Tampines St 82
SEAN AW
Blk 238 Yishun Ring Rd
SENG HAN TING
Blk 220 Bishan St 23
SERAPHINA LUM CHARMAINE
Blk 34 Telok Blangah Way
SERENE CHAI HUI LING
Blk 142 Yishun Ring Rd
SERENE KWEK SI LING
Blk 631 Ang Mo Kio Ave 4
SERISOPHIA
SHAHUL HAMEED
Blk 171 Woodlands St 11
SHANKARI
SHARON TAY SOCK LYN
Blk 251 Hougang Ave 3
SHAUN
Blk 486H Tampines Ave 9
SHAWN CHUA
Blk 170 Bt Batok West Ave 8
SHERRY
Blk 61 Lengkok Bahru
SHERYL WONG
SHIRLEY CHONG SUET LAI
Blk 57 Sims Dr

SHIRLEY JAUIER MIRANDA
  Mugliston Rd
SIAH AI LEEN
  Jln Teratai 1/1, Taman Bt Teratai, 56100,
  Kuala Lumpur
SIMON LAI XI WEN
  Blk 241 Bishan St 22
SITI SABARIAH BTE ABDULLAH
  Tyersall Ave
SITI ZUBEIDAH BTE KADIR
  Blk 427 Tampines St 41
SITI AISHAH BTE HAMSARI
  Blk 320 Jurong East St 31
SITI NORWAHYU BTE HANAFI
  Blk 52 Chai Chee St
SITI NUR AISYAH BTE KASMANI
  Blk 43 Pandan Gdn
SONG MING JUN
SONYA T
  Mulberry Ave
STEPHANIE NG CHIA CHIA
  Blk 116 Ang Mo Kio Ave 4
SULAIMAN BIN RAHMAT
  Blk 517 Jelapang Rd
SULIANA BTE JOHANI
  Blk 321 Bt Batok St 33
SUNITA KAUR
  Blk 462 Pasir Ris Dr 10
SUNNY OU
  Yishun Ring Rd
SYAMALAN SUBRAMANIAM
  Jln USJ 4/4C, 47600 Subang Jaya,
  Selangor Darul Eltsan
SYED AZLI BIN SYED ROSLI
  Blk 646 Yishun St 61
T. RAJPRABU
  Blk 427 Serangoon Central
TAMMY ANG
TAN
TAN CHEE SHENG
  Seria 7000, Brunei Darussalam
TAN CHEN KEONG
  Tmn Desa Mesra, Tmn Desa, old Klang
  Rd, Tmn Evergreen, 58100, Kuala
  Lumpur
TAN HAI ZHEN
  Blk 46 Bedok South Ave 3
TAN HENG CHAI
  Blk 295 Bedok South Ave 3
TAN HUI JUN
  Blk 173 Yishun Ave 7
TAN KAI LIN
  Blk 113 Pasir Ris St 11
TAN LITING

TAN MEI ANN
  Jln Ibus, Southern Pk, 41200 Klang
  Selangor
TAN MING HUI
  Everitt Rd
TAN PENG CHENG
  Blk 318 Jurong East St 31
TAN SEN CHONG
  Blk 230 Chua Chu Kang Central
TAN SHI HUI
  Blk 219 Bt Batok
TAN WEI CHEN
  Blk 542 Ang Mo Kio Ave 10
TAN WEN HAN
  Jln Permas 8/2 81750 Masai Johor Bahru
TAN YIK HOE
  Blk 611 Woodlands Ring Rd
TANG HING TUNG
  Jln Muhibbah, 96000 Sibu, Sarawak
TEO BOON HUI
  Blk 131 Marsiling Rise
TEO KOK YEE
  Blk 127 Bedok Reservoir
TEO POR TAO
TEO SOCK HOON
  Blk 29 Havelock Rd
TERENCE ONG KIAN WAN
  Blk 465 Pasir Ris St 41
THIRUMURTHY RAO
  Blk 241 Yishun Ring Rd
THOMAS THAM CHEE LEONG
  Blk 3 Hillview Ave
THOMAS YANG YUAN JUN
  Blk 849 Jurong West St 81
TOH CHIK WEE
  Blk 131 Ang Mo Kio Ave 3
TOINI YVONNE KUTAI
  Lor 1, Taman Ridge View, Phase 9, 88200
  Kota Kinabalu, Sabah
TRICIA LI ZHEN HUI
  Blk 838 Tampines St 82
VALERIE TAN
VANI
VERNA LOO MEOW CHIN
  Blk 627 Bedok Reservoir Rd
VICTORIA TING
  Lor Foohow No. 1, Taman Three Hills Pk
  No. 1, 93300 Kuching, Sarawak
VINCENT CHEN WEIDE
  Blk 11 Joo Seng Rd
VINCENT CHUNG
  Lot 2623 Jln Pateh Berbai, Seria, Brunei
  Darussalam
VINCENT GOK

Blk 529 Jurong West St 52
VINCENT TEO T S
VISHNU DEO RAI
  Chua Chu Kang Central
WAHID RAHIM
  Blk 442 Ang Mo Kio Ave 10
WALTON SEAH JUN RONG
  Blk 413 Ang Mo Kio Ave 10
WANG KAIREN
  Blk 224 Bishan St 23
WILLINA
WILMA DUCOSIN
  Philippines
WINNIE CHU LIJUAN
  Lucky Gdns
WONG KEET YAN
  Blk 10 Ghim Moh Rd
WONG SONG LING
  Blk 102 Bedok North Ave 4
WONG TAO KIM
  Blk 666 Yishun Ave 4
WONG WENDY
  Blk 404 Tampines St 41
WU PEICONG
  Blk 927 Yishun Central 1
YE XINZI
  Blk 119 Teck Whye L
YEO JENNY
  Colchester Gr
YEOW PUI SHAN
  Blk 542 Chua Chu Kang St 52
YI YING
  Blk 326 Serangoon Ave 3
YIP SOK YEE
  Jln Pasar, 83000 Batu Pahat, Johor
YONG SIAK MENG
  Blk 257 Boon Lay Dr
YU MING HONG
  Blk 838 Hougang Central
YUES YASUDAS MATHEW
  Jln Kuras
ZHANG FUMIN
  Blk 449 Bt Panjang Ring Rd
ZHANG FUWEI
  Blk 449 Bt Panjang Ring Rd
ZHANG KANGYI
  Blk 353 Chao Chu Kang Central
ZHAO ZHENG YOU
  Blk 5 Marsiling Dr
ZHOU ZIYAO
ZULIANAH BTE ZULKIFLI
  Blk 29 Marsiling Dr

Don't be disappointed if you didn't win a prize. Try again. Remember, a letter to us means your name will be in this book, in cold print, forever.

Occasionally, we've trouble handing out the prizes because no contact details were given. So don't forget to include yours. Write soon! I'll be waiting...

russelllee@flameoftheforest.com

CONTENTS

PART I

PART II

RUSSELL LEE INVESTIGATES:
HUMAN SACRIFICE

PART III

PART IV

RUSSELL LEE INVESTIGATES:
KALI, THE BLACK GODDESS MOTHER

PART V

PART I

"PUAKA" PEOPLE

Rahim Sidek, 72, retired fisherman

Have you ever seen "puaka" (Malay for "nature spirits")? My friends and I spotted them often in the open spaces near rivers in the old days.

The sightings usually happened when we were returning home to our kampung after fishing or when we were going out to sea. The puaka looked like tiny human beings, no bigger than the size of a Coca-Cola bottle.

They usually came out in the open very early in the morning, emerging from the ground at the foot of the trees. We watched them from behind bushes. They were playful and we could even hear them laughing.

When we placed morsels of cooked rice, eggs and fish near where they emerged, inevitably, the food would disappear.

Now, more than 50 years later, a lot of land in the area has been cleared for development and many of my friends have passed on or become too old to go fishing.

However, you can still see the puaka if you rise up early, but only from a distance. They disappear if anyone comes too close. The puaka seem to have diminished in numbers. I wonder where the others are.

I do miss them but I guess economic development will not wait — even for puaka people.

KARAOKE TO DIE FOR

Johnson Tan, 24, salesman

We always go to the same karaoke lounge, off one of the lorongs in Geylang. The girls are very pretty and their gangster friends are showing off the whole night.

My friends and I are salesmen. Maybe this is as close to living dangerously as we will ever get! And my friend, Cedric Chew Ah Teck, knows this little house in the back lane where the mamasan gives him a special deal.

When we went there one night, the place was almost deserted. Just the mamasan and her girls, and an old man. We'd heard him sing before. Ai-yoh, low-yah! He had a squeaky voice and he always ran out of breath half-way through the song. Very painful.

We ordered our drinks and the girl Cedric liked was rubbing up against him. We felt pretty good... until the old man got up to sing.

"Oh no," we groaned.

Sure enough, he staggered up to the microphone and called out for Number 66.

The next minute we heard the beginning of the song that everyone tries to sing: "My Way".

The old man must have been very drunk. He flopped down onto a stool, loosened his tie, and launched into the opening line.

"And now, the end is near..."

But instead of his usual terrible voice, he sounded different. The hair stood on the back of my neck. I blinked. I couldn't believe what I was hearing.

I swear, it was the voice of Frank Sinatra coming out of the old drunk's mouth!

Everyone in the bar had stopped talking. We just stared at the singer.

"I took the blows…"

Sinatra's voice sang on and on. The old man was sweating. His face had grown grey. He was standing now, one arm outstretched just like Sinatra when he sings.

"I did it my… way…"

As the song ended, we all stood up and clapped. We had never experienced anything like it. And as we cheered, the old man's eyes blinked once, then he fell forward, onto the floor.

He didn't move. We rushed over, rolling him onto his back. But it was too late. He was icy cold. He was dead!

The mamasan threw a sheet over the still figure on the floor. She closed the bar and we went home, whispering to each other about what we'd seen and heard.

I reached home feeling very disturbed. I flicked on the television and froze. The announcer was interrupting the programme with a news flash.

"Frank Sinatra died tonight in Los Angeles at the age of 82…"

My skin was tingling with fear. That old man had certainly sounded like Sinatra. Had the singer's spirit possessed him, just for one more rendition of "My Way", before it passed into the next world?

And then, when I woke in the morning, I saw a short story in the paper.

"An 82-year-old man collapsed and died in a karaoke lounge in Geylang last night. He was identified as Mr Frank Sin."

Russell Lee: Frank Sin had to go... but did he do it his way or was it Sinatra's way? By the way, Damien Sin wants to make it clear that Frank is no relation of his.

THE DEADLY DOCK

Richard Wee, 21, undergraduate

Before I had left Singapore for an American university, Russell, I read some of your books. I didn't believe any of it!

So, Russell, I hope you'll forgive me, because something happened in New York that really changed my mind.

Some friends and I had gone to New York for the weekend. We went out drinking on the Saturday night. At around midnight, my friends said they were tired and they left me alone in a bar on the Lower West Side.

I don't know if you've been to New York, but that part of town can be very dangerous. The streets are very dark, lined with old warehouses, the kind of area where trouble looks for you.

When I stumbled out of the bar into the windswept, deserted street; it must have been one o'clock in the morning. There were no taxis. After all that drink, I felt a bit dizzy so I decided to walk for a bit.

I'd gone a couple of blocks when I realised I was lost. For some reason I decided to turn the corner. Suddenly my skin prickled and all my hair was on end. I had reached the Hudson River. I froze, staring at the derelict docks, the last traces of the bustling waterfront where all the big ships had once steamed into port. Now the docks were abandoned, just ruined buildings shrouded in shadows remained.

The wind was howling across the racing waters. I shivered. And in that instant I heard someone shouting for help. The pleas became louder and more desperate. It was a woman.

I hurried towards the nearest dock. It was high tide and icy black waves slapped at the rotting timbers. The screams were closer. Up ahead in the murky light I could see something white, struggling in the water.

I picked my way across the creaking planks. There, beneath my feet, the moonlight revealed a terrified face.

I've never seen a face more exquisite. Her high cheekbones and finely sculptured nose were perfectly elegant, framed by the raven black hair plastered to her head.

"Help me! Save me!" she wailed.

I knelt down, carefully clasping a beam of wood to support my weight, and stretched out a hand. Her fingers were like ice as they gripped my hand. I hauled with all my might and she struggled up onto the dock beside me.

I gasped. She was clad in a thin white dress, but not an ordinary one. It had an old-fashioned look, like something out of a movie, quite long and stitched with lace.

"Let me call a doctor," I suggested, "or an ambulance. You must be freezing."

She seemed to ignore me. Her blue eyes widened. She choked out a question, "Is… is this New York?"

I was alarmed. Something in her manner struck terror in my heart. I stepped back.

"Y-yes," I stammered. Was she mad? I wondered. New York was supposed to be full of weird people!

Suddenly she leapt up, her long wet dress whipped tightly around her slender body by the bitterly cold wind. For a moment she looked like a trapped animal… then she ran off.

I tried to follow her but almost lost my footing on the old dock. By the time I reached the street she had vanished.

I heard a laugh. I spun around. There was an old black man, crouched in the ruins, holding a wine bottle. I edged towards him.

"Excuse me," I asked, "did you see a woman run past? A woman in white?"

The black face laughed. It didn't look friendly.

"Not again," said a slurred voice. "Always on nights like this…"

"You've seen her, too?" I demanded. "Who is she? Where did she come from?"

The black man waved his bottle and pointed. I followed his gaze. There was a faded signboard over the dock. I could just make out the lettering "White Star Line".

"All the big ships came in here, man," said the old drunk. "All except one. The one she was on. It never reached port."

I must have looked puzzled because he laughed, swigging from the bottle.

"Hey, man, ain't you never heard of the Titanic?"

FLOWER CHILD

Jasmine Seet, 13, student

When my parents did well in their business, they bought a nice double-storey bungalow in Seletar Hills. It was painted all white, except for the insides. My room was on the upper floor overlooking the garden. And that is what I like best about the house — the garden.

The several bougainvillea plants and their bright red and pink flowers lighted up the whole garden. Two jasmine climbers filled the morning with their natural perfume. But the most beautiful part was the flowerbed at the back, where there were orchids and other flowers growing.

"It's a mess... silly girl!" my mother said, when I told her about the flowerbed. "We'll get the gardener to fix it when we are settled, okay?"

"Mess? But it's nice. I don't care, I don't want anyone to fix it... I'll fix it myself!" I said.

"That's good, Jasmine. I hope you mean it — don't lose interest after a while..."

Sometimes, it makes me so angry when she treats me like a child! But I was determined to give the garden tender loving care.

I borrowed books on gardening from my school library and began pottering around. I took out the weeds and watered the plants diligently. In a matter of months, the garden became even more lovely; it was my pride and joy.

One day, while weeding, a flash of reflected sunlight dazzled me from within the undergrowth. I picked up the object and brushed the dirt off. It was a set of tiny seashells, a little silver bell and a blue ribbon... they were all tied together on a piece of black string like a necklace.

I felt I was holding something special and magical. I wore it around my neck.

When I did this, a gust of wind blew, shaking the tops of the trees, causing them to shed their leaves. I shivered. The sky darkened. It was going to rain, so I went into the house.

I washed the necklace. Some of the mud and grime had sunk deep and it took some hard scrubbing to get it all off.

The necklace looked even prettier after the cleaning. The little silver bell tinkled and sparkled. The small seashells, I saw, were special. They were all the same size and shape but different colours. I felt I was wearing a rainbow around my neck.

However, more and more, I was sure it belonged to someone else! One day, I put it in the drawer of my desk and forgot all about it.

That same night, while I was slipping into

sleep, I was awakened by a tapping sound at my window. I woke up with a start; the window latch came unfastened and something big, dark and hairy pushed itself into my room.

I was about to scream when I saw it was only the branch of a tree. It had rained during the day, and the night was windy and cold. Just when I was about to close the window, I felt goose pimples rise on my arms.

My hand froze on the window latch; it was stuck. I looked out into the darkness and heard the soft muffled sound of bitter weeping...

"Who's there?" I said, gently.

At that very instant, the weeping stopped. I managed to close the window and went to sleep.

The next day, a Saturday, I woke up with a fever. My mother took me to see a doctor and I had a temperature of 40 degrees!

"Nothing serious, just rest," the doctor said.

What a waste, to fall sick on Saturday. I spent all day indoors. I didn't do any gardening at all.

That night, I was awakened again by the same tapping at my window. When I went to the window, I saw a milky white hand... tapping at the window pane. And behind that hand, a ghostly pale face with deep, shining eyes, like black pearls, looking me in the eye!

I screamed.

"It's just a nightmare," said mum after she had come rushing in.

"But I saw a face... I really saw it!"

"It's the fever, darling..."

Mum said she would sleep with me but I declined her offer. Like I said, I hated to be treated like a kid.

Early Sunday morning, everyone went to church except me. I was ill and the rest made me feel better. It was a very nice Sunday morning. I went down to my garden.

I checked on the changes I had made. It wasn't much, but I had hung some chimes on the branches of the trees and installed a birdbath.

"O, no... don't tell me it's going to rain again?" I groaned because the sky had darkened suddenly. But when I looked up, I noticed the unnatural silence all around me. All the wind chimes that had been tinkling musically, were still. And though not a trace of wind shook the trees, they began shedding again, but not leaves this time...

Flowers. The trees were shedding their flowers. They fell softly and gently, like a curtain of snowflakes, the red bougainvillea among the pools of petals stood out like blood. It all looked so beautiful that I wasn't scared when I saw the face I saw in the window again.

She walked towards me, silently, slowly. So thin and pale, she looked as fragile as the petals of the flowers. She wore a simple white cotton frock with lace trimmings. She had long, straight, black hair that hung down to her waist. It was such beautiful hair, soft and shiny.

I didn't like her. She looked stuck up and proud. When she got closer, my heart melted when I saw her face up close... a pretty and delicate face. She looked lonely; it filled me with an unbearable ache of tenderness and compassion. She looked at me… and immediately… I knew!

"O, no!" I gasped. And then I ran, my heart thumping loudly, as I raced up the stairs to my room.

"Please wait! Don't go," I called out from my window. I yanked open my drawer… there it was, just as I had left it! I ran back to the garden.

"I'm sorry, I didn't know; this is yours, right?" She smiled.

"Right."

Her voice was as soft and musical as the wind chimes. And under the cool shade of the trees in my garden, on a big rock covered with green moss, we sat and talked.

She said her name was Rosemary. She was my age and she used to live here. And that was long, long ago…

When I gave her the necklace, she put it on immediately. How pretty it looked on her!

"Where did you get it?" I asked.

Her hand shot up and touched it protectively as it nestled on her bosom, on the lace trim of her white dress. She looked away, a little self-conscious and shy. She said she had made it herself, after she met "him".

"He" was Rudy, whom she had met in Penang. They had found the shells together and Rudy had painted them. The blue ribbon was what she wore in her hair on the day they met.

"What about the silver bell?"

"O," she laughed and said, "it belonged to Tom, my cat. I kept it and carried it everywhere with me after he passed away… and on that day at the beach, I had lost it. But it was Rudy who found it for me. It was so sweet of him! I didn't even know him then! We became friends after that."

She told me the story of her romance. I listened intently and didn't even realise it when my family returned.

"Why are you sitting out here all alone? You're not well you know?" my mother said, eyeing me suspiciously.

"Why are you looking at me like that?"

"I heard voices, who were you talking to?"

I turned back to point out my new friend but when I turned around... she was gone.

The next day, when I got back from school, I was in a panic when I saw some workmen digging up the flowerbed in the garden.

"Don't worry, Jasmine. They're only doing it so we can have a swimming pool!"

"No!" I yelled at mother. "No! Stop! Stop it!" I screamed, running out towards the workmen.

As I approached the garden, the men stopped work and backed off, away from a gaping hole in the ground. Something they saw had frightened them. Whatever it was, my garden was ruined.

When I reached the edge of the large hole they had dug, I saw exactly why they had stopped work...

In that hole, where the flowerbed used to be, there was a complete skeleton of a young girl about my age and size, and around her neck, there was a necklace... of tiny seashells, a blue ribbon and a silver bell!

By the end of the day, they had everything cleared away. I told my parents about Rosemary.

A priest came the next day and performed some rituals. I told my parents that there was no need for priests... Rosemary wouldn't hurt us. She was given a proper burial. Would Rosemary really have preferred it this way? I wonder.

The garden is much smaller now with the swimming pool in place. I am growing to be fond of the pool, swimming in it often. At times, I feel I'm not alone. Even when there's nobody in the pool, there are ripples on the surface of the water...

HELL RIDER

Eddie Chan, sales manager, 43

My story is set in the Seventies, when I was a teenager. I was quite "havoc" then, with long hair and I rode with a motorbike gang, the Hell Riders.

Of course, the Hell Riders were pretty tame and harmless. More like a "club" than a "gang" actually. But in Singapore, I suppose a little notoriety is necessary for a bunch of young people who are looking for a good time.

One of the highlights of our activities was the weekend cross-country races with other motor gangs. It was during one such race that I had this ghostly encounter.

I guess I was pretty lost that Saturday night when it all began. I somehow got separated with the rest; too much beer along with the MX pills I took. I was starting to get double-vision. And to make matters worse, I rode into a police road block in the Lim Chu Kang area!

And though I was high, I was clear headed enough to realise I was in trouble.

I slowed down, and headed to the side of the road where the police indicated.

The cops looked like they meant business. And people like myself, long-haired bikers, were their favourite targets! And what's more, it was a Saturday night.

But just as I was about to stop, I remembered... I still had a bottle full of MX pills on me! In my panic, I kicked my machine into high gear and sped off. The cops were stunned for a moment... a very short moment... and then they gave chase.

My Yamaha RD-20 had been extensively modified. Unfortunately, all the modifications were for looks instead of speed; the cops were gaining on me! Images of the rotan and jail were already in my mind when, up ahead, I saw another biker wearing the same colours of our gang. He signalled me to follow him.

We turned into Jalan Bahar cemetery and managed to shake off the cops. When I saw him turn off his lights, I did the same. Straining my eyes to see in the darkness, I followed him down a maze of winding paths, far from where the road turned to gravel.

However, I kept turning back, to check if the cops were still following. When I saw their blue lights flashing and heard their sirens fade as they headed off in the wrong direction, I was so happy, I took a fall.

But I wasn't badly hurt. Just a few scratches. As I inspected my bike, the rider up ahead parked in what looked like a familiar spot. Then he headed towards me.

Hearing the crunch of his motorcycle boots on the gravel in the darkness of the graveyard gave me an eerie feeling. Though I saw his jacket and knew he was in our gang, I didn't know him personally.

His hair was even longer than mine! When he took off his helmet, it flew in the wind with a lustre.

"Thanks for your help!" I said. I held out my hand but he declined to take it. I would have taken this for being aloof, but not from him... He wore such a serene expression, it was impossible to be offended. He said his name was Danny. And now I was sure I had never seen him before. If I did, I surely would have remembered, for he looked a bit like Wang Yu, that cool! No joke!

I found that I couldn't restart my bike.

"Hey, that's no problem. Take mine!" he offered.

"What about yourself?" I asked.

He said he would be all right. He was meeting his girlfriend here and they'd be spending the night at her place nearby. I felt another eerie feeling, looking around, it was all darkness! How could anyone be meeting up here?

"Danny!"

I was startled as a girl's voice called out. I was even more surprised when I saw her. She was beautiful! However, together now, they looked so sad and unhappy, as if there was so much weighing down upon their glamourous shoulders. I was eager to leave them alone.

"Just use my bike… you can return it tomorrow," said Danny. His attention was elsewhere.

"Thanks!" I said, and kick-started it. His motorbike came to life with a roar and I sped off with the wind in my face.

However, at this point, I felt a terrible lethargy come over me. I just couldn't keep my eyes open. I had to pull over and rest my eyes; otherwise I was sure to crash!

Unfortunately, when I closed my eyes, the MX and beer really kicked in and I slept till morning.

When I awoke at daybreak, I had the shock of my life. I found myself sitting astride a tombstone in the middle of Jalan Bahar cemetery!

Immediately, I got off and when I did, I happen to see the photo on the tombstone. It was a picture of Danny! And on the tombstone right next to his was a picture of his girlfriend; the girl I saw last night!

I read their inscription and saw that they had been engaged to be married, but both perished in an accident.

Such a shame, what a nice couple. Even as ghosts, they did no harm but helped a stranger in his hour of need.

BLOODY SECRET

Michael Lui, 36, unemployed

For 12 years, I worked as a carpet cleaner. All along my aim was to go into business for myself.

But not any more! Russell, I resigned last week. I had to escape from the hell which was taking over my life.

It all began when my boss sent me to a condo in the posh Meyer Road area. It was very new, very luxurious. I rang the bell at the Tay apartment, and this tai-tai let me in.

She seemed a nice lady. Beautifully dressed and groomed, Mrs Jennie Tay was the kind that played mahjong daily and shopped non-stop. I could also tell that she was the dominating type. And you certainly wouldn't want her as an enemy.

The Tay apartment was two-storeyed, with stairs up to the bedrooms. At the bottom of the stairs, Mrs Tay pointed to a dark red stain.

"My little dog died there," Mrs Tay told me sadly. "My maid was very naughty. The dog tried to bite her because she was stealing my money. She threw him down the stairs and killed him."

She was almost in tears and leaned against me for support. There was nobody in the apartment then. I can still remember the smell of her perfume to this day.

I examined the stain. The dog must have broken its skull, or been terribly injured, because a lot of blood had soaked through the carpet.

"Don't worry," I told Mrs Tay, "I will do my

best."

My assistant was ill that day, so I had to do the work myself. I applied the chemicals to the stain, then started the machine.

After an exhausting hour, the stain was completely removed. I rolled up the power cord, feeling satisfied over a job well done. I was about to write out the invoice when I happened to look down at the carpet again.

Russell, I swear I had cleaned it! But no, the stain was there again, worse than before, a darker red stain, and it looked wet. Like freshly spilled blood! I rubbed my eyes — it couldn't be! One minute the carpet had been perfectly clean. Now it was splashed with fresh, thick blood! Impossible!

I could even smell blood! But it wasn't dog's blood — it was the familiar scent of human blood!

I switched on my machine once more and applied more chemicals. This time I worked like a madman. I scrubbed and scrubbed; I worked the chemicals into every fibre of the carpet before finally using the vacuum.

At last, the carpet was totally clean, as good as new. I stood there, my whole body trembling.

And, as I watched, inch by inch, the red stain formed once again before my eyes until the carpet was saturated with even more blood than before!

I'm not religious but at that moment I uttered every prayer, every mantra, I'd ever learned in my life. I was shaking like a leaf.

The pool of blood began to move about, as though it had a life of its own. I then heard a muffled scream from beneath the carpet. My heart was thumping. I couldn't speak. There, before me, in the centre of all the wet, shiny blood, a face was coming into focus, horribly bruised and battered.

It was a young woman, and her voice screamed at me accusingly: "Why do you wash away my blood?"

"I am the victim," said the voice. "They killed me, their maid. It was Mrs Tay and her husband. They beat me up and kicked me down the stairs. I died in my own blood!"

I fell tack against the wall. Something, some instinct deep inside my brain, warned me to look up. Thank the gods I did! For there, racing down the stairs towards me, was Mrs Tay, no more the nice tai-tai, but a woman choked with evil, her face twisted with rage, a knife in her raised hand.

"So now you know," she screamed as she came nearer.

I fumbled for the door handle. I thrust it open, leaping out into the corridor. Mrs Tay's mad, echoing screams were ringing in my ears. I ran to the fire stairs; it was too dangerous to wait for the lift.

I rushed down the stairs, all 12 floors. And I kept running till I reached my van. I drove out into the street, past the security guard, all the way home.

I'm still on the run, Russell. I have rented a room in a hotel in Johor and I'm hiding out here, in case that mad woman finds me.

If she killed her maid, then she would think nothing of killing me, too.

Russell, one day I will go to the police, I swear

I will, but who would believe my story? Me, a poor carpet cleaner. What would my word be worth against rich Mrs Jennie Tay and her husband? And who would believe me if I told them of the dead maid who spoke to me?

One thing I do know: the maid's blood continues to cry out for justice.

A SPECIAL STORY

Russell Lee: We'll end this first section with this next story about Alan, a kind-hearted stranger. But there was more to Alan than meets the eye...

THE THIRD EYE

Melanie See, 29, veterinarian

It's been almost two years since I met the stranger that affected my life in a profound way.

The meeting took place in unlikely circumstances. It was in the middle of the night and I was taking a walk in town after a late night show. I heard someone shout "Look out!"

I turned around towards the direction of the voice and before I knew it, I was knocked down onto the City Hall sidewalk.

"Get off me!" I gasped, struggling to wrest myself free from the stranger who had pinned me to the ground. But he was strong, and far heavier than he looked.

"My God!" I thought. What was this mad man

trying to do to me? Here in the open as well! I doubled my efforts to break free, but he held me down with gentle ease.

"Shhh…" he said, with a smile. He was strikingly handsome.

I was confused at this point… I smiled… and then there was a loud crash. A window cleaner's gondola had fallen, crashing right smack on the spot where I had been standing!

"You must be extra careful this time of the year, miss," said the mysterious stranger. "It's the Hungry Ghost Festival. The spirits can become mischievous when they are let out to play."

He was charming and looked sophisticated. And yet he seemed serious about ghosts.

"Sorry," I said and giggled.

"That's all right," he said.

"Are you Singaporean?" I asked, and felt foolish for asking such a lame question. But I felt compelled to make conversation. I didn't want him to walk away from me.

He said his name was Alan — this mysterious stranger that saved my life.

As we walked together, I kept thinking that I would wake up at any moment to find that it was all a dream. Alan was tall, young and so handsome that everyone turned to stare at him when we passed by.

Alan's hair was long, soft, silken and shiny, like something out of a shampoo ad. It was cut in a most unusual way with a floppy fringe that covered his forehead. It looked childish, and a little girlish as well. But Alan wore it well. He had an air of elegance; classic and timeless.

In fact, Alan wasn't like a stranger at all. I felt comfortable with him.

That night, I took him home.

I live with my mother. My parents separated when I was only 13. My father left us for his mistress. I was confused and developed a general mistrust for men.

Teenage years came and left with no boyfriends, no dates, no romantic walks by the sea, no first kiss. I missed out on a lot. All my energies were focused on studies. I opted to be a vet because I love animals; they are honest and unpretentious, unlike people.

Mum often enquired about my lack of boyfriends. She was afraid I'd end up unmarried. My stock reply was I'd rather be a spinster than marry a man like father. But I stopped saying that because it only made her cry.

That night, however, my mother was delighted to meet Alan. However, she wasn't happy that he stayed the night.

Nothing happened, not at first. We went to my room and talked. I talked, actually, and he listened. He was a good listener.

And so I told him... everything. He listened and nodded. He not only understood me, but he could also see all the loneliness. What happened next was the most natural thing in the world. And it made me feel like a natural woman.

Afterwards, I couldn't sleep. I was basked in

the tingling afterglow of these wonderful new feelings.

I stared at the cracks in the ceiling, finding a world of wonderful details I had never noticed before. I stared at the familiar surroundings of my room and saw how love had transformed it. I stared at my sleeping lover, silent and serene...

And I screamed.

"What? What happened?" Alan spluttered, awaking suddenly. The fine features of his face had an eerie unnatural quality in the moonlight — an unearthly alien beauty, like something waxen and bloodless. Indeed, his expression was emotionless.

Looking at him, my shock and fear turned to a kind of deadly fascination. Slowly, the horror of it all gave way and I began to accept the facts... whatever it was; that glimpse of madness I got in the moonlight, I was determined to overlook it.

"Nothing," I said, "it was just a nightmare." And maybe it was. But there was something else I had to face up to, something I had been dying to ask at the very start, something that I simply had to know.

"Why Alan? Of all the other girls, why me? After all, I'm... I'm not... beautiful."

I wrenched out the question like a little piece of my heart. Alan winced. He felt both the pain of my asking and the pain that made me ask.

"It doesn't really matter, does it?" he replied, after a long pause.

He ruffled his hair and looked me in the eye, saying, "I don't care about looks because beauty is in the eye of the beholder."

And that was good enough for me.

Over the next few days, Alan would come and go mysteriously. Often, he would show up in the evening at the SPCA where I worked.

While waiting for me, Alan would walk around the area where the stray dogs where kept. If no home was found for the strays, they would be put down, a part of the job I disliked.

The dogs, I felt, were able to "sense" their predicament. And when a human is in sight, the dogs know it is life or death for them. They bark and howl like there's no tomorrow.

However, Alan had a strange effect on all of them. They grew quiet and peaceful when he walked the rows in between their cages. He seemed to have a calming effect on them, even as he searched thoroughly amongst them.

My mother continued to hate him though. Ever since Alan started to live with us, I stopped going with her to church. She tried to persuade him to go though, but with little success.

To make matters worse, he started to lecture my mother about a "faith healer" she had planned to see.

"He's a fake. Better see a doctor instead about your tumour," he said in earnest.

I thought mother would lose her temper. Instead, she gasped and stared in amazement.

"How you know I got a tumour? Melanie told you, is it?"

"Err... something like that," he stammered, the first time I saw him tell a lie.

That night, I pressed him again... about his past, his identity.

"Forget it Mel, you don't really want to know."

But I did. I felt hurt by the secrecy. I wouldn't stand for it. And so I told him to leave.

"All right," he sighed, and made to leave. It broke my heart but I wasn't going to stop him.

"Before I go, I think I'll tell you something I think you deserve to know."

"Just get it over with."

"Do you remember," he frowned thoughtfully, biting his underlip, before going on, "do you remember seeing this?" he said, brushing the long hair off his forehead.

I saw... and remembered.

"Get away... get away from me you freak... you devil!" I screamed.

"Sssh," he said, with a soft smile. The same soft smile that had enchanted me two weeks ago.

"Come on Melanie, climb off that table and put that ash tray down. You're not going to hit me with it," he said.

I calmed down a bit. And his story began...

"I am Er Lang Sen, the three-eyed general of the Jade Emperor of Heaven."

"Sure you are."

He went on. "Well, it doesn't matter whether you believe it or not," he said, slightly irritated. "It's a well-known Chinese legend! What's the matter, have you never read 'Journey to the West'?

Or at least watched the movie or TV adaptation?"

"O, yeah... I remember watching something on TV about it. But it was kid stuff!"

"What you mean 'kid stuff'? Don't you remember anything about it?" he said, looking angry for the first time.

"Not much really... all I remember is the Monkey King and the Pig," I said, really trying hard to remember, and giggling a little. I giggle when I get nervous.

"Melanie," he said, more solemn and serious, "if you make me fed up, I'm going to have to show you my third eye again."

"NO! Noooo... Please don't!" I cried.

"Is it... so bad?" he asked, looking hurt.

I thought of the first time I saw it that night, thinking it was a nightmare... that slit in his forehead, with no eyelashes or eyelids, just an eye as large as a pigeon's egg. Surrounded with unearthly white iris and a liquid black pupil that seemed to stare right into your soul.

"I keep it shielded from mortal eyes... it's just something I can do. After all, I am Er Lang Sen, the three-eyed general of the Jade Emperor of Heaven. If you'd given more attention to the classics, you'd remember I was sent to cage Sun Wu Kong."

I was numb, my head reeled from all this.

"I'm here on earth now because my dog... remember my dog?"

I shook my head.

"Tch... what's the matter with you, don't you know your Chinese history?"

I told him all that stuff was legend and myth — not history. He shook his head sadly.

"Ahh... you mortal girls can be so heartless." He looked hurt. And I began to feel sorry for him. I understood him completely, but I think he knew I didn't believe a word he was saying. But he continued with his tale anyway.

"During the time when that Stone Monkey, Sun Wu Kong, proclaimed himself to be The Great Sage, I was summoned to quash that revolution and cage the naughty Monkey. But I failed, you see, and Sun Wu Kong battled his way right up into the Celestial Gardens of Eternal Peace. That ape was really out of control! He left one third of Heaven in smoking ruins."

I could see that Alan was trying to shake off the memories in his mind. Memories clear, lucid and fresh. As if it all happened yesterday, and not 4,000 years ago.

"Of course," he continued, "the Jade Emperor was not happy about it. I was demoted from my lofty post to a lowly menial job. With all my powers, my skills and my all-seeing third eye, I was made to oversee the annual spirit crossing of the Seventh Lunar Month. What you call the Hungry Ghost Festival. My job is to ensure these restless souls pass from one world to another for their 'holiday', and back again when it's over. My trusty war dog was reduced to being a sheep dog for these wandering spirits. Every year the crowds got bigger, and this year, my dog got lost in the rush of that vast multitude... that's why I have to find it."

When he finished his tale, his pale face took on a waxy glow in the soft dim light of my room. It shone with an artificial inhuman perfection. I saw now how Alan looked so... unreal! But... Er Lang Sen? How could it be? And then I remembered — I did see that third eye on his forehead.

Whatever he was, he saved my life. And I still tingle from lingering sensations of warmth and tenderness from his touch.

"So, now that you know, do you still want me to go?"

I told him to stay.

My mother came back from the doctor's with some bad news. That tumour of hers was advanced cancer. The doctor said her days were numbered and that an operation was necessary. It would be costly. Painful too.

Mother and I were in despair. We were both shocked and appalled by Alan's opinion.

"Don't operate," he said. "You're going to die anyway. Better spend the time at home."

There was a moment of stunned silence. And then to my surprise, mother agreed!

She said Alan was right, she had led a full life and she didn't want to end her days in hospital with strangers around her.

At the end of the week, Alan's lost dog was found. It had wandered into the SPCA. Alan was happy, but there was a tinge of sadness as well. I guessed the reason for the heavy heart.

"I'll be leaving soon... not now, but soon," he said calmly and evenly. He tried to be a man about it and concealed his real emotion. But though his eyes were dry, tears trailed down his forehead from behind his long fringe.

He didn't say when he would have to go, but we both knew it would be at the end of the Hungry Ghost Festival.

Meanwhile, I had to prepare for another departure; my mother's. I made a point of being very close to her as the end drew near. We really bonded like never before. I remember, on her last night, she was saying how nice and cool the weather was. It was a rainy night and she was saying how she liked to sleep without air-con to enjoy the cool weather. She never woke up.

Alan didn't go to the funeral. The Hungry Ghost Festival was coming to an end, and he was preparing to leave.

However, when I got home, Alan... Er Lang Sen was gone.

Somehow, I just knew it. Although the Hungry Ghost Festival had not ended, I suppose he had left early to spare me from saying goodbye.

And it was goodbye. Goodbye to my mother, to my first romance.

As the wind blew away the remaining ashes of burnt offerings on the final night of the Hungry Ghost Festival, my mind was full of thoughts. The night breeze enveloped me as I said a thousand farewells. Again, no tears. I felt free...

I suppose Alan and I will meet again, in the end.

PART II

RUSSELL LEE INVESTIGATES:
HUMAN SACRIFICE

One of the most horrific practices in the occult world is the ritual killing of humans. Contrary to popular thinking, this practice is still rife. My research shows that specific demons are behind these barbaric acts. These demons first showed their presence in ancient Canaan and their influence quickly spread to Africa, India, Europe and America.

The origins

The beginnings of ritual human sacrifice to appease spirits can be traced to early history when the two daughters of Lot (the patriarch Abraham's nephew) slept with their own father! The descendents of the two sons of that forbidden union were called the Ammonites and the Moabites. Archaeologists have now discovered that both these nations worshipped Baal and Moloch. They are, in fact, one and the same god.

The wife of Moloch is called Ashteroth and the wife of Baal is Asherah. Ashteroth and Asherah represent the same fertility goddess. To the Greeks, this spirit was known as Aphrodite while the Egyptian version was known as Isis. Among all these peoples, it was believed that only a pure, bloody sacrifice would be sufficient to appease these spirits. For the ancients, this meant a child or a virgin.

Both Baal and Moloch worship indeed involved the ritual slaying of newly-born children and instances of these occurrences have been recorded. As I have explained in my earlier books, the life of a man or animal is in the blood and the spilling of blood is a necessary sign of the sacrifice of a life. So the bloodletting of virgins and children, symbolic of all that is pure and innocent, show the genuine and whole-hearted approach of the worshipper towards these diabolical spirits.

Carthage burial grounds

A historical survey shows just how rampant the ritual killing of humans was.

In ancient Carthage, altars used to kill children have been unearthed. Even the stone carvings in the area show scenes of children being butchered. Also found were clay jars used to hold the remains of the killed children. The extent of the killings is surprising for the burial grounds are quite large.

The people of Carthage are descendents of the Canaanites and their gods were Baal and Moloch. They knew the demon as "Tanet". Historical accounts describe mothers wailing for their infants and the drums beating loudly so as to drown out their cries.

The Aztec and Mayan holocausts

Although the Aztecs of Mexico were an advanced civilisation, they were notorious for their ritual killings. When the famous Great Temple was dedicated in 1487, priests butchered thousands of people in one day. Most of the rituals were conducted on the top of Aztec pyramids.

One Spanish conquistador reported finding a rack containing about 136,000 human skulls, all ritually murdered. The horrified Spanish massacred the Aztecs in response and tore down their temple. In its place, they built a cathedral.

The ancient Mayans, on their part, had several versions of human sacrifice: among the well-known ones were the "arrow sacrifice", the "heart sacrifice" and the "well sacrifice".

In the arrow sacrifice, a prisoner of war was paraded through the city, stripped naked, painted with blue paint, and tied to a stake. A priest proceeded to cut the prisoner and danced together with onlookers as blood gushed out. At a signal, each man shot an arrow at the victim's heart as he passed by.

The Mayans were famous for the heart sacrifice. The victim would be placed atop a pyramid before the heart was ripped out, placed on a plate and given to a priest. The body, which would be thrown down the pyramid, would be skinned, dismembered and eaten by priests and nobility.

The well sacrifice was the most merciful of the three. A victim was bound and thrown down the well. However, after a fixed time period, he would be rescued if he were still alive, a sign that the gods had spared the person.

Witchcraft and child sacrifice

The word "witchcraft" is commonly associated with the Salem witch trials. But the first "witches" were so called because they indulged in the practice of child sacrifice. That is why there is an injunction in the Bible: "suffer not a witch to live". This death penalty is for the murderous practices of witches, not for casting spells or making magic potions, most of which was ineffective anyway.

The commonplace idea of the witch casting spells and concocting potions is not quite accurate. The witches who were put to death in the Middle Ages were victims of gross superstition.

17th century France

Madame de Montespan, the mistress of France's King Louis the 14th, was a true witch. She was a worshipper of Ashteroth, wife of Moloch. It was eventually discovered that she ritually killed babies, procuring such children from prostitutes and the very poor. More than 2,500 babies were destroyed in this manner.

Nazism

The holocaust of the Second World War remains as one of the darkest spots of human history. More than six million were killed for racist reasons. It still boggles the mind that a tragedy of such massive proportions could take place. Yet, it was a sterilisation law passed in 1933 that began the systematic persecution of Christians and Jews in Germany. The sterilisation practice is linked to the worship of the goddesses of fertility.

Hitler believed that the Aryans could only be restored to their greatness if the purity of the race was re-established. Rules were made to stop marriages between Jews and non-Jews. Aryan couples who failed to procreate were fined. Abortion was encouraged for non-Aryans and illegal for Aryans. 400,000 ill and weak Germans were sterilised. Marriage was forbidden for those who suffered from hereditary problems. Breeding centres were set up for the elite. Women were also encouraged to have children outside marriage.

The Nazi leader behind all this madness was Heinrich Himmler, whose secret aim went beyond eugenics; what he really wanted was to create an Aryan religious order, with links to Aryan mysticism and the fertility goddesses. It eventually led to the genocide of the Jews.

Abortion

Abortion is a medical holocaust; it is today's most prevalent form of human sacrifice. Although abortion and human sacrifice are not identical, the reasons for both can be similar. Millions of babies are aborted all around the world every year because they are "sub-humans", the very same reasoning of the Nazis.

When a doctor wrenches out a foetus from a womb, and cuts it up, he is spilling the blood of a human. Make no mistake about it. Even if the courts allow it, it's still morally wrong — legalising the killing of infants doesn't make it all right.

My research shows that the gods Baal and Moloch are behind the abortion movement of today. It's human sacrifice in a disguised form.

Of course, I realise that sometimes the situation can be very delicate and often the reasons for abortion can be compelling. My point is that life is precious. And life begins in the womb — ask any mother. So please avoid putting yourself in a position where you are pushed into a corner. If you have to decide whether to abort or not, please seek help. Don't do anything stupid. Confide in a friend or call a help line. There are so many.

In the 17th century, European colonialists were shocked at the extent of the savagery of the African natives.

Human sacrifice was a norm: tribes would select scores of young girls, and raise them as vestal virgins. Pampered and adorned with finery, the girls were oblivious to the terrible fate in store for them.

On a special day, they would be brought to the village square and impaled on sharp long poles, to die a slow, painful death while the rest of the village gathered around to celebrate. This was a fertility rite, to ensure a good harvest.

Human sacrifice and cannibalism went along together among the tribes. These same tribes made slaves of their warring enemies and bought and sold them — for food!

The cannibals tortured their victims before consumption. The bones of victims were carefully broken, their skin skilfully peeled off, and their broken and flayed bodies immersed in spices and seasoning over a period of three days. They were to be kept alive throughout, until it was time for them to be cooked and served. Why? So that the meat was served "fresh"!

Animal sacrifice

Human sacrifice has its roots in animal sacrifice. The earliest animal sacrifices were symbolic of human sacrifices although no humans were killed.

In Africa, several times a year, on special holidays, the Bantu and Yoruba natives "celebrate" with a ritual animal sacrifice: a goat is slaughtered by a method known as "the 200 cuts". This sadistic execution is a protracted ritual of pain, where the animal is slowly skinned alive, with 200 cruel cuts before a final slash of the throat, the 201st cut, releases the animal from its agony. While the goat suffers, the worshippers loudly "celebrate" the ritual as they smear each other with the blood of the animal.

The new gods: Money, Lust and Self

Human sacrifice in the guise of abortion is still rife today. We sacrifice these lives because of three demons which we call "Money", "Lust" and "Self". More and more, however, the gods are being called by their proper names: Aphrodite, Baal, Moloch, Isis, Asherah, Ashteroth.

Every time a baby or human is killed, these gods become more and more powerful because the spilling of innocent blood does release power. Which explains the increasing influence of the abortion movement and the fertility goddesses.

A SPECIAL STORY

Russell Lee: The next story-teller has already told two stories (in Book 8 and Book 9). This is his final story and explains to a large extent why he is a tormented person. He has dabbled in the worst forms of the occult but has survived to tell us all about it. But he has had to pay a heavy price for his mistakes. A very heavy price.

MOLOCH

Anonymous, 74, retired civil servant

Russell Lee: Your two stories, "The Devil's High Priest" in Book 8 and "The Black Mass" in Book 9 attracted a lot of attention. Some readers even want to meet you and help out in any way they can.

There is little that anyone can do for me. Thank them anyway. I have to battle these demons alone.

I know you are trying to help. Just telling the two stories have been therapeutic, believe me.

Russell Lee: Do you have another story? I speak for many readers.

There is one deep and dark secret. Even the memory of it sends my head spinning and my heart pounding. I feel weak and I imagine that I am on the brink of everlasting damnation where the devils are eagerly preparing to torment me.

I deserve all that is waiting for me! Hell's opening its jaws, waiting to swallow me up. I am hanging by a rope above the hot flames and the twines are slowly unravelling.

Russell Lee: But what could have been so tragic that there is no forgiveness? Perhaps there is a way out.

It's probably the worst chapter of my life. Back in the 1940's, I joined a coven of witches in England. Back then, people imagined that witches were an extinct species. How wrong they were.

I joined the Wiccans, a group known for its witchcraft. Most of its members were female, between 21 and 35. We were secretive about our meetings, which were few and irregular anyway.

When a new member was initiated into the congregation, absolute loyalty was demanded. In the initiation rites, animals were killed and even menstrual blood was used for effective spells and for invoking the dark powers. But not every member was a witch. You had to have the spiritual "qualifications".

The meetings were often held in hidden, forested areas, away from the public's prying eyes. Drugs and alcohol were used and lovemaking was not uncommon. The idea was to be in touch with the earth's natural forces.

The High Priest or leader of the group was Aaron, a tall man, built like a bulldozer. He had a no-nonsense approach and was supremely confident that he had all the answers. I had both fear and respect for him. The others treated him as though he was a god, especially the women who were willing to do anything to please him. And that meant even giving him their bodies.

His motto was, "If it harms no-one, do what ye will." He spoke of the god called Moloch.

Russell Lee: As I have mentioned, the appearance of this god, Moloch, can be traced to the time of the Canaanites who practised child sacrifice. The ancient Israelites were influenced by the Canaanites and became promiscuous through the worship of Baal and Asherah.

Moloch demanded human sacrifice. In the Bible, it's recorded that the people "caused their sons and their daughters to pass through the fire to Moloch" and that "they burned their sons as an offering to Baal".

Moloch, a Hebrew word, means "to ascend the throne".

And just like it was in those days, so it is now. The sexual revolution of the 1960's has led to millions of babies being aborted every year. Abortion is now viewed as a fundamental right. Herein lies the connection between abortion, child sacrifice and witchcraft.

Aaron encouraged music and dance, love and free sex. He discouraged us from having just one partner. We should "have all things in common", he said. There was one very rich lady who sold all her possessions and gave millions of pounds to Aaron.

Anyway, there was a sprightly woman, Anna, in the group whom I grew fond of over time. It pained me to have to "share" her with others and I think she felt the same way. Her short, curly, golden hair and roundish face fitted well with the cavalier spirit she had. And when she smiled, her whole personality lit up. The whole world lit up for me. We tried to be together as often as we could.

Then Anna became pregnant. I was in a quandary. The baby was mine! I had never been married and never had a child before. Even though this child was unborn, I immediately felt a special affinity towards it.

"Aaron said that I should abort," Anna said to me one day.

"Forget it!" I blurted, not realising that I was directly challenging Aaron. Both of us were relatively new to the group and we didn't know that abortion was a common practice.

"A foetus is not human," Aaron said when he

got to know about Anna's condition. I listened in shock.

"It's my child! Mine!" I said limply. Anna was completely confused. She felt that she was a mother and sought to "protect" the child but the influence of the group and Aaron was very strong as well. She had been indoctrinated so deeply by the group that she was incapable of making any decisions on her own. Everything was decided for her.

We had to give up everything if we wanted to be in communion with Moloch, Aaron said. Even our children. That's why he had stressed that we shouldn't be possessive.

Now things were beginning to make sense. For him to promote free sex, he had to cover up the fruits of this activity. And that's why he allowed babies to be killed. I later heard that Aaron would even kill newborn babies in ritual sacrifice. The thought sent shivers down my spine. I planned to escape with Anna but she was petrified of Aaron. Foolishly, she decided to do the "honourable thing" and ask Aaron's counsel.

It was the wrong move. A big mistake.

"No! How can you break our code of loyalty!" Aaron thundered. "It's the bastard boyfriend of yours that's putting these thoughts in your head!"

Aaron confronted me. His sheer charisma overwhelmed me and I backed off. I was young then. Aaron knew he could bully me.

Aaron took full advantage of our weakness and said that the baby was a hindrance to our fellowship with Moloch. The best thing that we could do was to offer up the child as a sacrifice to Moloch to show our allegiance to the god. It would be a test. It would also release so much power that we could then become witches in our own right.

I didn't think that he was serious about it until I heard from the others that infants were occasionally slaughtered!

As Anna was in labour, the bastard Aaron prepared to kill the child. A circled pentagram was drawn and an altar set up as incense swirled and candles burned. Long sharp knives were laid on the altar in preparation. A silver, ornate chalice stood in front of the altar.

"MOLOCH! MOLOCH!" Aaron called out in invocation. "Come forth from Hell and share with us thy power! Give us all that we desire for we worship you!"

Meanwhile, the drums sounded and the trumpets blared. It was a very sure sound. Although the music was loud, it couldn't drown out the piercing wails of a woman in her birth pangs. But there was no joy as she finally gave birth to a man child.

I watched in horror and disbelief as they brought out my child, all bloody and umbilical cord still attached. A woman brought the child to Aaron. Anna rushed out, inspite of her weakened blood-drained body, to protect her child. As she approached Aaron, two men restrained her. She knew. Anna knew what was going on here.

Her plaintive cries were drowned out by the drums and the shouting all around. "My baby! My babeeee!!"

I swung into action. I grabbed hold of a wooden pole and stuck it right into Aaron's stomach as he doubled up in pain.

"BASTARD!" Aaron shouted and pointed at me. Immediately his lieutenants moved in. They were too strong for me. Too many of them and too strong.

"You SWINE! I'll kill you! Don't hurt my child!" I cried as the blows rained on me and darkness enclosed me.

When I came to, I was tied up and I saw Aaron holding up my child with outstretched arms. The worshippers cried out in unison, "MOLOCH! MOLOCH! MOLOCH!"

The moon was full, the gathering gloom foreboding. Even in the dark you could see the storm clouds assembling above, as if the heavens were protesting at this gross wickedness taking place on earth below.

I just couldn't believe what was going on right before my very eyes. Storybook stuff, not real life. And it couldn't be happening to me. I still could hear Anna's pitiful pleas in between the beating of the drums.

The child was placed over a basin, its throat slit and with a stifled cry, warm blood drained into a cold chalice.

The rain began to fall, the tears of heaven. I wanted the earth to open and swallow me up. Aaron then flung the child callously into the fire which had been burning all along in front of the altar.

Suddenly, the whole area was abuzz with energy. It may be that I was delirious but out of the fire came a beast-man. It had the head of a man and the body of a goat. Its eyes were as fire and its visage terrible. As it raised itself from the midst of the fire, it must have stood 12 feet. A thick fur covered its body and its voice was as the sound of many ocean waves.

"Worship me!" it bellowed, almost a growl. This was none other than the terrible, blood-thirsty demon Moloch, in the flesh.

Aaron looked on in sheer terror. He didn't expect his invocation to be answered in so tangible a fashion.

The demon lifted the child and swallowed it whole. With a swipe of its gigantic tail, many of the worshippers were sent crashing to the ground. I could see fear even on Aaron's face.

Moloch was satisfied, saliva drooling down the sides of his mouth. He moved towards Aaron, the ground shaking with each step he took. The rest of the worshippers ran off in all directions.

Just as he reached the High Priest, someone tipped over the chalice in all the chaos and the blood spilled onto the altar. Moloch stopped in his tracks and began to disappear slowly.

It was the blood. The blood of an innocent had given him the power to incarnate himself. But when the chalice had been tipped, and the contents spilled over, he lost that power. But my child was lost. Forever.

Anna just lost interest in life after that and died of a heart attack about a year later. Aaron was murdered within a week. Someone pumped six bullets into his body while he was sleeping.

Many others in the group died mysteriously. Although unspoken, most felt that Moloch was behind it all.

Until now, the picture of my child's throat being slit and his cries pierce my brain, every night. I can never erase the picture of Moloch swallowing my child whole.

To this day, the blood of my baby and Anna cry out to me. I feel that I killed my child and Anna as well. I was so irresponsible. In my thirst for special knowledge, I was reckless. And I continue to pay the price for it.

I joined the British Army soon after that. I completely gave up interest in the occult. The experiences in the Church of Satan, the Druids and the Wiccans were enough. That was more than 50 years ago.

After the war, I joined the civil service in Singapore. I'm retired now.

One more thing, Russell. I don't think I will be seeing you anymore. I feel that my end is near and I had better prepare myself. I hope against hope that I can find some comfort and solace in my anguish before I am no more.

Russell Lee: Goodbye, my friend, goodbye.

PART III

SILVER BELL

Stella Tay, 18, student

My grandmother would sometimes sit for hours at the window of the room I shared with her.

"I am feeling the spirits of those who have passed on," she explained to me.

My frown prompted her to explain: "You can see as well as feel spirits. Have you ever felt your hair standing for no reason? Or that somebody is watching you? That's what I mean. For example, when I sit here by the window, I can feel your grandfather's spirit. He is happy where he is but misses us. I wait for him to signal me and I come here to sit by the window to be with him."

Oh yeah. Right. Tell me another one.

"The signal? What signal?" I asked, pretending to be curious. I didn't want to hurt the old lady.

She smiled. "Do you see that little bell on the altar? Well, when it rings, I know he's here."

I looked at the little silver bell before the statue of Kwan Yin, the Goddess of Mercy. It was resting on a piece of yellow cloth. I said to grandmother, "But someone would have to lift the bell and shake it before it rings." I just couldn't help myself. How in the world was a statue going to sound the bell?

"Yes, of course. How else would it be able to make a sound?" she said.

"When does grandfather visit you?" I was playing her game. What to do, lah? Amuse her.

"In the afternoon," she said. Poor woman.

"For how long has this been going on?"

"Two years… since grandfather passed away."

"Why didn't you mention this before?"

She laughed. "I didn't want to scare anybody." She added softly, "Besides, Stella, some people might think that to believe in ghosts is ridiculous."

I felt myself blush.

I made up my mind to hang around our room in the hope of hearing the silver bell ring. The thought thrilled me. After all, the spirit was that of my grandfather.

I wasn't afraid. I had a quick lunch on my return from school the following afternoon and sat near the altar in our room, my eyes and ears alert.

"You didn't believe me when I told you about the bell, did you?" grandmother said as she sat by the window.

I didn't reply. How could that bell ring without anyone touching it? But I kept an eye on the bell.

Half an hour went by… then I saw the bell move… and I heard a gentle tinkle! No mistake about it — it did ring!

When I looked at grandmother, she was smiling.

Russell Lee: He who laughs last laughs best.

PASSENGER FROM HELL

Gregory Rozario, 56, taxi driver

They say taxi drivers see more things than anyone else. More weird things, more crazy things. Well, that's true. If you really want to know the truth about a city, ask a cabbie.

After 20 years behind the wheel of a cab, I thought I'd seen everything. Even those women who are desperate for men, the ones who offer you money to turn off the meter for a while and ask you for more than a ride home!

But there was this one night which even you, Russell Lee, will find hard to believe!

The rain was sheeting down, the wipers were slapping from side to side, and the tyres were slipping on the wet, greasy road. I'd just dropped off an old lady in Opera Estate and I was dying to relieve myself — must have been the sight of so much water. I took a short-cut through the back streets, heading for an all-night petrol kiosk on Upper East Coast Road.

I found myself cruising along Woo Mon Chew Road, with rain lashing my cab, drumming so loud on the roof I couldn't hear myself think. On a normal night, Woo Mon Chew is a nice little road, lined with neat, expensive homes. But that night, with the rainstorm in full force, it had a dark, menacing look. And I soon found out why...

From under the shadows of a giant tree, about half-way down, a man was hailing me. He must have been pretty frantic, his arms were waving like crazy. I started to apply the brakes, nice and easy, so I wouldn't skid into a storm drain.

As the figure grew closer, I was startled. It looked so familiar. Like someone I'd known for years. The way the man was built, and the clothes he was wearing. I couldn't see his face because of the tree, so I was wracking my brain to think who he was.

I looked again, through the swishing wipers. Hell! He was wearing my shirt, my trousers, same colours exactly. Even the way he stood was like the way I did. I thought I was seeing things!

The cab had drawn up beside him, and he stepped out from under the tree. I gasped. It was me! It was my face! I was sitting in my own cab, watching myself walking towards me!

Then, suddenly, before I knew what was happening, his head blew off — just like that! I saw my own face, my own head, separate itself from my own body, and go rolling down the gutter.

But it didn't stop him — oh, no, he just kept walking towards me, one hand reaching out for the door.

I screamed. I hit the accelerator and the cab leaped forward, skidding crazily, as I tore off down the street.

I looked into the rear-view mirror but the street was empty. It was only when I swerved madly into Upper East Coast Road that I realised I'd wet myself. But do you blame me?

When I reached the petrol kiosk, I lurched out towards the toilet.

There was more drama in store for me.

"Greg, you're alive!" It was one of my best friends. Another cabbie ran up and grabbed me by the shoulders. His taxi was parked by the side of the kiosk.

I must have looked stunned. I just stood there, letting the rain beat down on me.

"Half an hour ago, on the taxi radio, I heard your voice shouting for help. You said you were being attacked by a passenger! Then a few minutes later, they found your cab, and you were inside it. Your head had been slashed off!"

I must have fainted.

When I woke up, there were about a dozen drivers and the police, all staring at me, wanting to know what had happened.

To this very day, I just can't explain it. Yes, there'd been a mistake. It was another driver who had died. But, but what about that vision I'd seen — of myself without a head? How do you explain that?

Was it me who should have died that night?

Russell Lee: Most taxi drivers I meet have a lot of ghost stories to tell. Greg's is one of the more interesting ones I've heard.

THE TUA KONG ICE-CREAM MAN

Rafidah Abdullah, 39, clerk

I have never told anyone my story. It still haunts my memory at night, and I hope that by penning my experience, I can find relief...

I was born and raised in Jalan Tua Kong, near the shops at Siglap. In those days, about 30 years ago, Tua Kong was a notorious hideout for gangsters who lived in the old kampungs where the Hacienda condominium now stands. Jalan Tua Kong was just a winding lane, fringed with attap houses, old temples and outcrops of jungle.

Every Saturday afternoon, an old Malay man selling ice-cream would pedal his bike along the dusty track. When the children ran up to him, he got off his bike and opened the lid of his sidecar to dig inside for their treats.

I must have been 10 years old when I heard his bell ringing one particular Saturday afternoon. It was a sound I loved. He rang this old bell by hand, the sort they used in schools at the time.

I begged my father for some coins, then ran out into the lane. But instead of the old Malay man, there was a beautiful girl riding his bike. I guessed it was his daughter, perhaps taking over because he was ill or had gone away. Two or three of my friends also ran out to greet her.

She stopped ringing the bell, got off the bike and smiled at us.

"Durian, durian!" I called out my favourite flavour.

Her face was bathed in an expression of sweetness. Her eyes, as I recall, were jet black. She waved us closer and we huddled around the sidecar. Her long, thin hand rumpled my hair before it lifted the lid of her ice-cream container. I remember wondering why my hair felt so hot from her touch.

Then she reached inside the container. But she didn't pull out a durian ice-cream. Instead, up came the head of the old Malay man, his gory entrails swishing from beneath his neck! His blood sloshed everywhere.

As we jumped back, screaming and squealing, I looked into the girl's face. Her eyes now glowed like hot coals, red and orange, and her skin was radiating an eerie light. She tossed the old ice-cream seller's head into the air, its entrails dangling like a comet's tail through the sky.

We ran screaming and yelling to our homes. I shuddered, beads pouring down my face. I threw myself at my father, begging him to protect me. I told him what had happened and he ran to the door, but Jalan Tua Kong was deserted.

Later that day, he took me to a bomoh. I was told that the old Malay man had been captured by a pontianak. He must have met his fate near the Siglap cemetery because that was where they found the rest of his body. The bomoh chanted some special spells to safeguard me.

We moved away from Tua Kong soon after and settled in Jurong. But even to this day I can still hear that old bell ringing and ringing, ringing and ringing.

I pray that the pontianak will never find me.

Russell, do you think I'm safe after all these years?

Russell Lee: You are safe and sound now. Relax, have an ice-cream or something.

A WALK ON THE WILD SIDE

Kunawan, 37, businessman

Upper Aljunied Road must be the spookiest road in all of Singapore, especially the area just outside the Mount Vernon crematorium. There are cemeteries on both sides of the road and the lanes around this quiet area are bordered by huge trees. When darkness falls, this is a street you'd want to avoid.

My car happened to break down along that stretch of road one evening. While waiting for the tow truck, a blanket of darkness and silence fell over both sides of the road. The only sounds were made by creatures of the night and the occasional vehicle passing by.

Still, you sensed that there was a lot of "other kinds of activity" around. I couldn't trust my own senses and kept telling myself to keep cool. The stupid tow truck would be here real soon. Why the hell was it taking so long?

While staring into the darkness, I faintly heard someone — or something — singing ever so sweetly. I pointed my powerful, six-battery torchlight all around the area. I turned my flashlight upwards to the trees. There, perched on a branch high up, was a beautifully-coloured bird. It stopped singing and flew away.

I began to instinctively walk away from where I was standing towards a housing estate further down the road.

As I started to walk, the beam of my flashlight shone on the figure of a young and beautiful woman in a sarong kebaya. She looked shyly away, covering her face with her "selendang", head-scarf. She said sweetly in Malay, "Why don't you come with me?"

I was too impressed by her beauty to think that she could've been a ghost or an evil spirit.

My mind said, "Let's have some fun." So I eagerly nodded.

"Where do you wish to take me?" I asked, giving up any restraint. Even the picture of my wife in my mind couldn't stop me.

She replied, "To the tree, where it's romantic. Come, follow me."

She walked a few paces ahead, stopped and smiled. "Come on, don't be so shy."

She reached the tree first and then, my eyes popped out as she began to walk up the tree! In slow-motion! Then she stood upside down under a branch, looking at me!

"Come!" she said.

I think I must've broken the world record for the 100 metres!

Of course, I said nothing to my wife about what had happened when I reached home.

The next morning, I learned that the car had been taken to the workshop.

The tow truck driver reported to me that he had heard someone singing from inside my car all the way to the workshop. He imagined that it was my radio acting up.

I sold my car after the repairs were done and I always steer clear of Upper Aljunied Road.

THE LAST FLIGHT

Melanie Chua, 24, air hostess

I was in London after a flight from Singapore when I suffered an attack of tonsillitis. It was partly due to the stress of work.

It was so bad that I saw a doctor. He told me I needed an operation to have my tonsils removed!

"It's not serious," he said. "But just to be safe, I think you should do it as soon as possible, here."

That very evening, I checked into St. Martin's Hospital in the East End. Maybe I can meet a nice English doctor here like Richard Gere? Come on! Of course I know he's American! But an English version is okay with me.

That first night at St. Martin's was difficult. I found it hard to sleep. My own timing was all askew, due to jet lag. Besides, this place was really creepy at night! It was old, perhaps Victorian.

"Here luv," said the night nurse, handing me an assortment of tranquillisers.

And on that first night I dreamed I was back in uniform, but I was barefoot!

In my dream, I could feel the cold tiles as I wandered around in the departure lounge of a vast, shadowy airport. This airport was like no other I had seen. It was gigantic, everything looked way out of proportion. I am 1.7 metres tall, but the chairs in this place made me feel like a child. When I sat down, my feet couldn't reach the ground!

The scary part of the dream was that the airport was deserted. Not a soul around. It was also completely shrouded in darkness... The only light was from the moon; it seemed to float just outside the tall glass windows, overlooking the empty runways.

I was very fearful... I was walking round and round in endless circles. I was getting hysterical and started to run.

The maze-like corridors led me down one blind alley, and then another. I was breathless. Confusion and terror gripped me. The cold floor beneath me stung the soles of my feet. I climbed up and sat on a chair. And then I saw him...

I don't know who he was... either Japanese or Korean. He looked about my age. I wasn't so afraid now... he looked familiar! Like a movie star or a model. But he sat like a big dummy; he stared into space! Like I wasn't even there.

That's why I got such a fright when he turned to face me suddenly and smiled.

That made me frantic, I struggled to scream. But the medication kept me asleep. I was trapped in the dream.

When I did wake up, the sheets were all wet from my perspiration, the cold sweat of fear!

I was a nervous wreck the next day. And I was very happy when my colleague and best friend Juanita came to visit me.

"What's he like?" she frowned after I told her about my dream.

"What do you mean what's he like?" I rasped hoarsely, barely able to speak.

"I mean, what's he like? Handsome, ugly or what?"

"I don't remember," I said, though I think I did, and, I think she thought I did as well.

"Well, if you see him again, ask for his telephone number!"

I felt silly then, and thought no more about it.

On the second night, I dreamed again...

The same dream, right up to the point when he turned and smiled. But this time, I kept my cool and tried to talk. But when I tried to speak, I couldn't! My tonsils were in a worse state.

It was all so strange!

The following day was the day of the operation! Although it was routine, I couldn't shake off this premonition of dread and disaster!

I went out of my ward for some fresh air and just as I was going back to my ward, some of the hospital staff were taking someone to the intensive care ward.

As they passed me, I noticed that the guy was the very same handsome person in my dream! But he looked real sick. I was overwhelmed now by a tide of thoughts... what's going on?

I was to have my operation this evening. I wasn't to eat anything all day! However, the operation went smoothly.

That night I had another fitful rest. I was in the same dream once again.

The whole scene was very different this time. The mysterious airport wasn't empty. It was full of people. All kinds. But they all appeared to have something in common with each other — all except me. I felt excluded and alienated. Except for one person.

The mysterious handsome guy I had seen. In my dreams, and in the hospital.

"Hello," he said.

"Hi," I replied, amazed at how easily I was able to say it… then I realised — I had my tonsils out today!

We chatted for a while. He was really nice. Suddenly, everyone in the airport stood up and got ready to go. He, too, looked about and got ready with them, as if they all heard some announcement over the PA that I couldn't hear.

An acute sense of fear engulfed me. They were all going except me!

"Wait, take me with you!" I pleaded.

"No," he said smiling, "you don't really want to go where we're going."

"But how will I see you again? How can I contact you? Do you want my pager number?" I said. I couldn't believe how desperate I sounded!

"Ah, but unfortunately…" he said, a little distracted. Then he looked out of the tall windows, at the moon. Bigger and brighter than ever… as it hovered close, closer…

And above, there was the roar of a thousand engines, and a vast flapping of giant wings, as everyone in the airport stampeded in a mad rush of panic… and then the moon crashed in through the windows!

"NOOOOO!" I awoke.

Jumping out of bed, I ran, feeling the cold floor under my bare feet. I ran straight to the intensive care ward, bursting through the door, just in time to see the doctor pulling a white sheet, covering the face of the man I had seen in my dreams.

"Was he a friend of yours?" one of the staff asked.

And after a long, long pause, I replied, "Yes, yes, he was. A friend."

A friend who was on the last flight out.

JEREMY

Dorothy Chan, 64, retired teacher

For 21 years, I've heard the cry of a young lad coming from under a tree near where I live in Pasir Panjang. Thinking that perhaps I was ill, I consulted doctors, psychologists, bomohs, tangkis, taken magic potions and yet the cries continued. What was driving me crazy was that I could do nothing to comfort the boy.

Russell Lee, when I read the accounts of the supernatural in your True Singapore Ghost Stories, I felt that if I sent you my story, it might heal my feelings.

Anyway, the boy always "appeared" at about nine in the evening with his head buried in his chest and a deep, worried frown on his face. It was difficult to tell his nationality and he couldn't have been more than eight. At around midnight, he would get up and fade out of sight.

The lad was an enigma. Nobody knew who he

was. Some of my friends left food and candy beside the tree, but these were ignored by him. Some gamblers came to the tree to try and get "lucky" lottery numbers from him but they realised that the lad had no interest in making anybody rich.

I often wondered whether the boy could have been waiting for someone — a loved one, perhaps? A friend of mine, a psychic, decided to find out.

One morning, she sat under the tree and called on the spirit of the boy. An hour passed, but she didn't make any contact. It began to drizzle and as she was preparing to leave the place, she felt very strong vibrations — it was the boy's spirit! She spoke to him gently for a while. His name was "Jeremy".

The boy said both he and his mother had been killed in a car accident along Pasir Panjang Road a very long time ago. She had asked him to wait for her under the tree. So far, she had not shown up. He was sad and lonely and cried for her every day, he had said to my psychic friend. He would go on waiting for her and when she arrived, they would go away together.

My friend then attempted to call on Jeremy's mother to tell her of her son's predicament. The attempt must have been a success because from that time, there hasn't been a single sighting of the boy.

After 21 years, Jeremy was finally free of his anguish.

A SPECIAL STORY

THE PRINCE AND PRINCESS OF BEDOK

Jamal Bin Tahir, 24, student

About three years ago, when I was in school, a new girl joined my class. Her name was Lina. She was the most beautiful girl I had ever seen in my life. I mean it. She was even nicer than all the stars in movies, MTV, etc.

I know this sounds shallow and childish but everyone else in school felt the same way. Even teachers praised her... for qualities like manners, neatness, punctuality. Which was a sham! She was just an average student though she was in the "science" stream. And her behaviour was more or less like all the rest. Nothing outstanding... only her looks. The beauty made people see even non-existent qualities.

But not me though. I wasn't like all the other poor fools who fought among themselves over her. It was obvious to me that she couldn't care less for them. I was glad to see that she rejected them all, and she did it in a way that wasn't heartless or mean... just cool.

She had one quality I could see the others couldn't. Style.

I was also touched to see that she kept to herself mostly, in a way that said "I am an individual". I am like that as well.

And though she was friendly, she had no close friends. She kept to herself. And this quiet dignity gave her an aura of "class".

I too kept to myself. In fact, I hardly had any friends. It wasn't because I was stuck-up; just that I simply didn't share the same interests as others in my age group. And I didn't see the point of pretending to identify with a pop group or football team, just to be able to talk about them.

My parents were hard working; we were comfortable, not well off. I had hoped to make it to university. I had to work hard, I knew I couldn't depend on my parents, knowing I had two younger siblings dependant on them as well.

So I didn't have time for "social" activities.

However, suddenly, everything went very wrong... I felt my concentration slipping. I lacked focus and all my studies were on the slide. Although I passed the mid-term exams, my results were appalling.

And no matter how I tried, I just couldn't overcome the new distraction... she even stayed around Bedok, so even when I didn't see her in school, I knew she was never far away, always somewhere around the neighbourhood.

The distraction was the new girl, Lina. Some nights, I couldn't sleep at all. Usually, I took walks in the cool night air to soothe the feverish dreams in my mind.

I lived in Bedok Reservoir Road, in a block not far from the actual reservoir in Bedok. I liked walking there. It was very lovely there late at night. The wind whispered through the trees and the moon reflected its light in the shimmering ripples on the water.

However, some people thought I was mad. For I went there, unlike all the lovey-dovey couples, alone.

Late one Friday night, I was feeling particularly restless. I had already changed into my sarong and was ready for bed. But I could hear the music from my sister's room next door. And every song that the radio played... seemed to steal my heart away.

So I put on my track pants, a tee-shirt and my old Adidas running shoes. And went for a walk around the reservoir...

It was very dark that night, not a star in the sky. I could feel the moisture in the cold breeze. On the shadowy surface of the reservoir, the black waters bubbled and churned as if something was stirring in its depths.

Numerous suicides had taken place here. Also, this was the infamous place where the victims of the Bedok Rapist met their doom back in the 80's.

I looked at my watch and saw it was midnight already. And though I had no school the next day, I thought it best that I go home.

But I was unable to move. I stood rooted to the spot when I saw a strange light glowing beneath the surface. It made the waters swirl in a spiral motion which mesmerised me. The wind became stronger and blew a rising cloud of water vapour in my face. But I knew something was wrong when I saw the smoke on the water...

I saw a ghostly lady rise up and stand upon the waters. She stood quite a distance away, around the middle of the reservoir. I couldn't see her clearly, just the shadowy outline of someone tall and thin with long hair dancing in the wind.

And then she turned to look at me. From where I stood, I could see a pair of fiery red eyes.

She moved towards me... I was dumbstruck, and simply froze; I couldn't move.

However, she stopped dead in her tracks when she was about 10 metres away. The fire in her eyes now flickered. There was some uncertainty in her gestures that suggested confusion.

"Ahhh..." I heard her voice in my head. "But you haven't come here to kill yourself, have you? Why are you here? Why have you come to me?"

"I only came for a walk," I wanted to say but I was too scared to talk. I could feel her presence in my head, probing my mind. And then, I felt shame as I heard her mocking laughter.

"Ha ha ha ha ha!"

"What's so funny?" I said, surprised at myself.

"You. That's what's so funny! Your noble notions of love — true love! Ha ha ha..."

I hung my head in shame. For, in the face of this demon... in the face of sure death, in my mind... there was tucked away in a corner, the image of Lina Rahman.

"This is your lucky night young man! I will fulfil your childish dream! Just so that you can learn... the real nature of this wicked world!"

"Wha...what?" I mumbled. In the dark, I could see her raise one long thin arm, and the sharp claws of her spade-like hands as she tossed to me a small leather pouch with a drawstring. It landed on the ground in between my feet.

I picked it up and examined it. It was made of soft brown leather, like suede. It looked small enough to fit easily into any ordinary jeans pocket. And very light, as if all it contained was a handful of dust. But holding it in my hands, feeling the material of the pouch, I could feel the brittle metallic quality of the substance it contained. I could almost sense it was something rare and precious. Like gold or diamond dust. But just as I fiddled with the drawstring, I heard her voice booming…

"Don't touch that!"

I froze.

"Good… that's good, boy… I'm doing you a favour, you don't know it, but you'll thank me later. I warn you, once you open that bag, or spill even one drop of its contents — then it's all over!"

I couldn't explain it… but I knew, I just knew that this little treasure I was now stuffing into my pants was going to do me nothing but good. Just like… magic.

Since that wonderful night at the reservoir, everything in my life took off. My school results… it was so easy.

A few magazines I had written to in search of part-time work replied. All of them offered employment and the pay was far above my expectations!

I also received a letter excusing me from National Service! What a break! And, on the personal side, the thing with… you know… her. I mean Lina, well… let's just say everything fell into place naturally.

I was happy for a while... but only for a while.

Lina and I were quite a pair. We made a lot of new friends in the circles I moved in. Suddenly all the industry people wanted to know me and became friendly. The problem was all of them didn't know the real me. No, not even Lina.

So, one Friday night, when Lina and I were supposed to go to a party... I took her to Bedok Reservoir instead.

It was a clear bright night and the sky overhead was sparkling with the blazing white light of a million stars.

She squinted, batting her eyelashes as the cool breeze blew playfully into her face. She looked so beautiful that night.

"Lina, I... I..."

"What is it, Jamal?"

The sound of her voice uttering my name sounded remote and strange. Alien and unnatural. Something strange but I couldn't figure out what it was. Perhaps, it would be the last time that I would hear my name on her lips. And on a beautiful night like this, it was probably the best time to say goodbye.

I stammered, I stuttered and I wondered if I made any sense at all. It must have come out all confused. All the details. I found myself wondering about the reality of it all myself...

"I don't know if you believe me or not Lina. But it's all true... and this..." I said, showing her the leather pouch the apparition gave me.

She looked at it blankly. Even as I undid the drawstring and tipped its contents. Exactly what I thought at the start — nothing but a handful of dust. I threw the pouch into the water.

"This is it... and... I just hope you don't get angry, if you should ever think of me. And if you choose to forget me... I wouldn't blame you at all."

She looked at me in horror, staring at my face like I was a monster. I was surprised at first, but I realised... right now she was seeing me as I really was, for the first time.

"Yes, I think it's high time to stop the whole charade."

"Huh?"

I was puzzled, what did she mean? And then, she took out from her purse, a pouch with a drawstring just like mine! And she threw it into the reservoir as well.

"When my family just moved here, I was lonely and depressed, suicidal! And I came out here late one night too... and she, she came to me as well..."

She had her back turned to me as she spoke. And I saw... all the lustre and shine fade from her hair.

And then she turned around.

"Well, Jamal... I won't blame you too, if you choose to forget," she said. On her face was a wry smile, and her bright eyes shone as she saw the irony of it all.

I gasped, backing away in shock... nothing magical about her now. From the maddening beauty of the Lina Rahman I knew, now there was just... just... Lina Rahman.

But you know what?

Neither of us forgot. In fact, we both chose to remember... to this day...

Now, Lina Rahman is Lina Tahir, my wife. She is a princess to me.

Russell Lee: A fairy-tale ending... and may the prince and princess of Bedok live happily ever after!

PART IV

RUSSELL LEE INVESTIGATES:
KALI, THE BLACK GODDESS MOTHER

Kali, the Black Goddess of Dakshineswar, is a major figure in the Hindu pantheon of gods. Kali can manifest itself in both the benign and threatening form.

Dakshinar Kali

Dakshinar Kali is the popular, "mainstream" Kali, the benign mother goddess. Images and idols of the benign Kali depict her with her right foot forward, and her left hand holding a sword. Her visage is gentler and less threatening. The Goddess Kali here is a mother, a protector. People pray to this divine mother in the spirit of love and trust.

Dakshinar Kali grants boons to the wombs of barren women. She also ensures the welfare and well-being of the family, blessing her worshippers for their devotion with liberation — freedom from misery and suffering.

Smashan Kali

However, if the idol or image of Kali has her standing with her left foot forward and brandishing a sword with her right hand, that means it is the goddess Smashan Kali, the not-so-benign version.

She is the goddess of death, the mother of destruction. She is Kali of the Cremation Ground, on the black night after the doomsday, when all life on earth must end.

Most religions, including Christians, Muslims

and Jews, believe in a final day of doom and destruction for the world. "Armageddon" and "Apocalypse" are some of the common terms used to describe this event. The idea is a day when existence as we know it will terminate.

Lord Krishna revealed the coming of this terrible time, when he ended the Age of the Brahmins — the horror of the Age of Kali. And this is the age we are living in now.

When the whole planet is reduced to ruins of smoking ashes, and the earth is soaked from the blood of the dead bodies piled up in mounds, the vast and terrible silence of this abomination of desolation will be broken by the cries of joy from heroic Kali worshippers who have burnt away all worldly desires and seek nothing but union with her. These worshippers fear nothing and know no aversion.

Smashan Kali is the embodiment of the power of destruction, surrounded by corpses, ravens and jackals. Wicked female spirits serve as her handmaidens. From her mouth flows a stream of blood. Around her neck hangs a garland of human heads and around her waist is a girdle made of human arms. Her long luxuriant hair grows wild and free. Each strand is a "jive", a soul.

The Dakshineswar Temple

In the inner sanctum of the Dakshineswar Temple in India, there stands the Holy Shrine to Kali. Pilgrims to this inner sanctum, a mere 15 feet by 15 feet square on the vast grounds of the temple, bear witness to the fact that this basalt image of Kali has no shadow. For they say god does not cast a shadow.

Kali and her worshippers are sometimes misunderstood. Most religions have a belief that God is all good, and the Devil is all bad. However, Kali is the full picture of the "universal power". She is the benign mother and the terrible mother. By her, we see good and bad but she is neither. This whole world and all we see is maya, the veil of the divine mother. Kali is beyond good and evil.

This is not so hard to understand when we look at other forms of worship. Every religion that preaches peace and love, also preach death and destruction to non-believers.

The "Thugs" extremists

A noted extremist group which pledged allegiance to Kali existed around AD 800. The "Thugs", as they were known, worshipped Kali's terrifying form, Durga, wife of Siva.

About a million people are said to have been killed by the Thugs from the 17th to the 19th centuries. They were strangled with a twisted cloth, called kerchief, then hauled away for ritual mutilation of the bodies. This included the use of "Kali's tooth", a sacred pickaxe.

In the Hindu scriptures, the Shatapata Veda, it is written, "The sacrificer will sacrifice a man first for man is the first of all animals. Thus he slaughters the victim according to its form and according to its excellence". Perhaps the Thugs used this passage to try and justify their actions.

The British, led by Sir William Sleeman,

waged a "hearts and minds" campaign in the 18th and 19th centuries to turn villagers against the Thugs and recruited volunteers to hunt them down. Groups such as the Thugs have given the impression that Kali worship is connected with murder and violence.

Rumours of human sacrifice to Kali emerge in India from time to time even till this day but there are few confirmations.

Conclusion: A god in man's image?

The Thugs group is an example of how religion is misused. Men always have a tendency to give their own interpretation of what true religion is. But when they do that, they inevitably impose their own ideas on the truth. In a way, it's true that we sometimes worship a god we create in our own minds.

Religion, therefore, is what you make of it. It starts and ends in honesty. You can make god in your own image or worship a god that is divinely revealed, independent of man's imagination. The choice is yours.

So, ladies and gentlemen, boys and girls, bow down before the one you serve. You're going to get what you deserve…

A SPECIAL STORY

Russell Lee: Recently, I met up with one of Singapore's most colourful characters, Venga, the team manager of Woodlands Wellington Football Club. He didn't disappoint and told me this next story.

KALI'S GARLAND

R. Vengadasalam, 37, soccer manager

My friend told me this story a long time ago. Since then I've come to realise that many others also know about it. It's gruesome but true to the best of my knowledge.

A gang leader, Jumbo, who was violent all the days of his life, was lying seriously ill in hospital. This hospital, which shall remain unnamed, is in the Serangoon Road area.

The doctors didn't think that Jumbo would survive the knife wounds that he had suffered in a fight. Every night, he would toss and turn on his bed as his fever and pain grew worse.

Almost 60 stitches were needed to sew up the long and deep gash in his stomach. A lot of blood had been lost. But Jumbo was a fighter and he was not about to give up so easily. In his own way, Jumbo was a devout man and prayed to Kali, the goddess of death and destruction, for a recovery.

Jumbo's arms were lined with fine cuts; these were a testimony to his devotion to Kali. He offered his own blood as an offering to the goddess. Now, in his time of need, he asked for favours in return.

"Kali-ma, Kali-ma, KALI-MA!" he would say repeatedly. Jumbo felt that the goddess had delivered him many times and, now, she wouldn't fail him, no matter what. In return, she had his complete loyalty and devotion.

Jumbo's family members were allowed to

visit him. But they could do nothing to pacify him. Even from his hospital bed, he would get angry very quickly and spit out venom and promise vengeance against his enemies.

The police kept him under guard around the clock. He was a wanted criminal for a number of offences and they weren't going to let him escape.

One night, as it rained heavily, Jumbo yelled out in pain. The thunder and lightning sounded a warning of impending danger. Family members remember this night well for it was the night that Jumbo went missing from his bed.

They searched all night. Police cars and tracker dogs were used to comb the whole area. Eventually, they found Jumbo. In a nearby temple, lying prostrate before the statue of Kali, dead. Jumbo had ripped apart his wound and taken out all his intestines and hung them like a garland on the goddess before collapsing.

To this day, nobody is able to explain why Jumbo did it.

The garland around the idol with Jumbo before it must have been an awesome sight in the stormy night.

Russell Lee: If you live by the sword, you'll die by it too. For Jumbo, justice was done in the end.

PART V

THE FINAL STORM

Sally Wong, 16, student

I was the last person to see Kim alive.

We were running home from school in a terrible storm. Lightning flashed and thunder rocked our estate. We had reached the huge drain. Usually we scaled the fence and crossed over it along a narrow pipe, but that day the surging waters were slapping high against the sides and the pipe looked very slippery.

"Can! Come on, Sally, let's cross!" Kim had yelled, and before I could stop her, she was over the fence and on the pipe.

"No!" I screamed. "It's too dangerous! Let's take the long way!"

Kim ignored my warning. She edged along the pipe, her school haversack balanced on her back.

"Kim, please come back!"

But it was too late. She had reached the centre of the pipe when suddenly she lost her footing and plunged into the deadly torrent.

I clambered over the fence. All I could see were the raging waters. Kim had vanished.

I ran to the nearby hawker centre, screaming for help. Several men followed me to the drain while another rang the police.

Soon there were dozens of people around the drain, walking along the sides looking for some trace of my missing friend. My parents came and took me home. Later that night I heard that her school bag had been found a mile away, wedged under some debris.

For days, police divers checked the entire length of the drain. One of her shoes was found, at the point where the drain emptied into the sea. But her body wasn't recovered.

Day after day, her parents waited anxiously on the seashore. They couldn't believe their daughter was dead. Until her body was found, they could have no peace.

I became very depressed. Somehow I blamed myself for her death. I should have stopped her! I should have! But how? Kim was always breaking the rules, I knew that, and what could I have done?

The whole school attended the memorial service and as we left the chapel, a fierce storm broke out. I shivered. It reminded me of the day she disappeared.

And that was when a ghostly feeling took control of me. Something was telling me to take a taxi to the beach where Kim and I used to play as youngsters. I had just enough money for the fare.

I got out and walked onto the beach. The sand was wet. The rain beat down, throwing a curtain of water over the harbour.

"Not here!"

It was Kim's voice! I looked around, but I was alone.

"The jetty."

The voice again.

I crossed the sand to the long jetty. I climbed up onto the timbers and walked along it. I must have reached half-way when I heard Kim's voice again. It was a soft, sad sound in the back of my mind.

"I'm here. Please tell them."

I could feel her presence beneath my feet. It was the scariest moment of my life.

I ran back to the beach and called the police emergency number. I gave the location of the jetty. I told them there was a body in the water beneath it. When they asked for my name, I hung up.

I ran to the bus stop and spent my last coins going home.

That night, on television, there was a story of how Kim's body had been found under the jetty. The strong currents had washed it out to sea, then brought it back to shore. The police said they had received an anonymous tip from a member of the public.

I fell onto my bed, sobbing.

And that was when I heard Kim's voice for the last time.

"Thank you, Sally, my dear friend. Now I can rest peacefully."

PAK RAMLEE, TOK GURU AND SHAITAN

Iwan Maideen, 43, textile merchant

I grew up in a kampung in Sembawang. It wasn't so very long ago that the bustling urban estate of today was an idyllic rural village.

I must say, I miss those days. Life was simple then. People were friendly and cooperative. Neighbours genuinely cared for each other. Singaporeans, in general, weren't so materialistic.

However, there's always the exception to the rule. And in my kampung then, the exception was Pak Ramlee. His house was like a grand, luxurious villa compared to the humble simplicity of surrounding attap houses.

Pak Ramlee was a landlord and he owned a few shophouses that he rented out at a good profit. Despite all the money he was making, he also ran an illegal money-lending operation, with the aid of the "Samseng" (three stars); a Chinese secret society gang which was very powerful at the time.

As you can guess, Pak Ramlee was a very feared man. But he wasn't a respected man. And nobody liked him, too. It didn't bother him though. He only cared about money. The other concern of his was — fear.

For one reason or another, Pak Ramlee was a very superstitious man. He consulted a bomoh regularly. For what reason, no one was sure. But soon, because the bomoh appeared so regularly in our kampung, performing some foul ritual or another for Pak Ramlee, everyone knew him as well.

The bomoh, Tok Guru, was a burly guy. In his 30's, Tok Guru had long hair and his thick bushy beard was dark and oily. It was accentuated by the black clothes he wore.

Tok Guru was a dandy and exceedingly vain. He wore silver bangles on his wrists and a ring on every finger. The gold teeth in his mouth glinted whenever he smiled, but he seldom smiled. His bloodshot eyes shone with raging hellfire.

Late one Friday evening, I heard my father and uncles talking as they were returning from the mosque.

"Tch... dosa... dosa besar!" said my father, shaking his head in disgust.

"Betul, betul punya haramzada!" my uncle cursed, hissing angrily.

At that time, I was still innocent. A mere child. But even then I could feel their outrage. So I just kept my mouth shut and listened.

Later, I found out that Pak Ramlee's gangster flunkeys pressured a poor man who was indebted to him into committing suicide.

All because of a paltry debt. A gambling debt that he couldn't pay. And if that wasn't bad enough, the bloodsucker sent his poisonous people to dispossess whatever valuables the victim left for his widow and children. And though it didn't add up to much, there was something there that was intriguing. It looked like a real treasure... something priceless.

It was an old brass oil lamp, with Arabic inscription on it that no one could decipher. The victim had been a sailor when he was young and had picked up the item when he was in Mecca.

It was supposed to be lucky. Now it was in the hands of Pak Ramlee.

The very next day, the whole kampung was in an uproar. For something happened on the first night Pak Ramlee brought the lamp home.

No one was sure what had happened but all of Pak Ramlee's servants quit suddenly. Some of them left town altogether! Of those who remained, not one could explain their reasons properly. One poor fellow lost his mind completely. He kept muttering something about a "djinn".

The day after, there was an even bigger uproar when Pak Ramlee's four wives packed their bags and took their children with them. For what reason, none could say.

Pak Ramlee was seen in the village on that day of desertion. He wasn't heartbroken at all. Instead, he rejoiced.

"Eh... semua tak guna!" He accused them of being a pack of parasites who only wanted his money... but everyone he spoke to saw that Pak Ramlee wasn't his usual obnoxious self...

That night, the bomoh, Tok Guru, stayed at the big empty house while Pak Ramlee himself abode with his brother in town.

Bright and early next morning, Tok Guru came swaggering into town. Triumphant and arrogant, he boasted to one and all who would listen.

"Alamak... senang!" The braggart bomoh hoisted one leg up on a long bench he sat on in the coffeeshop, as a few people gathered to listen. Most of his avid listeners were indolent young men very much like himself.

"Djinn? Hah! Kuching kurap punya hantu! I ambik parang..." saying thus, he sprang to his feet and pulled his curved cut-throat blade, demonstrating a few flashy silat moves for the benefit of the girls looking on.

And though I hate to admit it, I was impressed as well. Everyone, though, seemed to have forgotten the circumstances that led up to this display.

However, it was far from over…

Tok Guru said that after fighting off the djinn, the spirit was not satisfied and said it would seek its master's help, to deal with him.

This caused a stir. Someone asked who the djinn's master was. The bomoh's bloodshot eyes grew wide, and replied dramatically that the djinn's master was Shaitan himself!

However, the braggart boasted he wasn't afraid, that he would deal with Shaitan the same way he sorted out the djinn. He even invited some of the youngsters to watch him in action.

They were scared of course, but the bomoh's confidence reassured them. And late that evening, as a low yellow moon hung in the sky, unnaturally big and bright in the darkening sky, a group led by Tok Guru headed off for Pak Ramlee's house.

As for myself? Of course I didn't go. But reports of the night's proceedings were consistent.

It was about midnight. Everyone in the house panicked when they heard the sound… of howling dogs, all the way from the Chinese kampung across the tracks. But Tok Guru told them to relax; this had happened the night before too.

The darkness seemed to intensify as a chilling wind started blowing… rattling the doors and windows of the house.

Once again, Tok Guru told them to relax, as it was a mere "action replay". At this point, the djinn appeared.

A glowing, childlike figure dressed in the court robes of ancient Arabia, the djinn looked like a cute little baby. But upon closer inspection, they saw it wasn't cute at all. For upon the childish body, there grew an oversized, leprous head of an evil, old man. Its skin was a filthy shade of yellowish white. And within its big red mouth grew sharp teeth, its black forked tongue flicked around its lips like that of a snake. Its golden eyes shone with ancient malice and cunning.

However, the bomoh was steady. He whipped out a black dog bone on a string of human teeth and chanted a magic spell.

This incantation held the djinn rooted to the spot he stood and rendered him powerless. But the djinn spoke.

"Don't be happy yet, bomoh! As I told you, tonight, my master's coming!"

Its black snake tongue dripped with green venom and its eyes flashed fire... the horror of its fury was nothing compared to the thought of the Master coming! The others trembled in anticipation, but Tok Guru was fearless.

"The harder they come... the harder they fall... Call your master! BRING HIM ON!!" the bomoh commanded.

The djinn closed its eyes and mumbled... The front door creaked open and Tok Guru struck with all his might. He knew he had to strike fast and strike first, otherwise the formidable foe would surely overpower him!

Swiftly and suddenly, the curve of his blade carved the air, as he slashed, striking the djinn's master's neck, severing it clean in one stroke and sending its head rolling onto the floor.

The moon appeared now, and its light flooded the room, along with the mocking laughter of the djinn.

Tok Guru's parang fell to the floor when he saw. The djinn had tricked him! It wasn't its master that was slain. It was Tok Guru's own master, Pak Ramlee!

Tok Guru was never the same after that. He lost his mind. The youngsters who accompanied him too suffered in one way or another.

In the meantime, the villagers restored to the widow the dispossessed personal items. It was a small comfort for the loss of her husband.

CECILIA AND SUNITA

Cecilia Ramasamy, 31, laboratory assistant

They say that good friendships last forever. I had one such friendship.

When I started my first day in kindergarten, I met Sunita, who was to become an important part of my life. She was a sweet little girl, insecure initially, but once we knew each other, we became like twin sisters. Whenever I needed her, Sunita was always there for me. And I vowed to be true to her too.

We went through Yio Chu Kang Primary School together, sharing our triumphs and heartaches. In fact, some of the other girls said we could read each other's minds. That's how close we were!

In Secondary One, our mums let us go to our first pop concert at the Indoor Stadium. Boney-M was our favourite band, and we sang out the songs together, screaming and waving with the others in the crowd. It was a great night and so we'd remember it forever, we gave each other a Boney-M tee-shirt.

It was shortly after that concert, on a Sunday night, when I was packing my bag for school, that my mum came into my room. She had tears in her eyes. I stared at her, puzzled.

"Cecilia, come here," she said, holding me close. "Sunita was knocked down by a car... she passed away."

I froze. The words echoed in my brain. Sunita? Dead? I couldn't believe it!

"It happened quickly..."

Something inside me snapped. I just collapsed, in a flood of tears. My mother held me tight, but there was nothing she could do to ease the pain. Sunita was dead. The girl who had shared all my hopes and dreams. Gone, without even a chance for me to say goodbye!

Suddenly my life was terribly empty. Nothing seemed to matter anymore. At her funeral, I felt like in a trance. My mind couldn't accept that Sunita was no more. Why? Why did God allow this?

The first weekend after her death was really bad. Sunita and I had planned to go to the movies, then a meal at Serangoon Road. I cried for hours at the thought of it!

A few kind school friends begged me to go out with them. Mum, too, said I should go.

"You must do something positive, dear," she pleaded. "Sunita will always have a place in your heart, but learn to make new friends…"

So I agreed to go — but Sunita would come with me! When I put on the Boney-M tee-shirt she'd bought me, I felt better immediately.

We were walking down to the MRT station when it happened. I suppose I was too busy thinking of Sunita to concentrate on what I was doing.

I stepped out onto the crossing, without checking the traffic light. I heard the screech of brakes. There were screams, too, voices calling out my name. Something told me I was going to die!

And then, Russell, some power, some invisible force, seemed to lift me away from danger. It felt like a gust of wind, blowing me back to the footpath, as a huge truck thundered past.

I was saved from certain death!

I clasped a hand to my heart, and knew that Sunita's tee-shirt was magic. Somehow it had spared my life.

Just as that moment, I thought I heard Sunita's voice again: "I'll always watch out for you, dear friend."

Russell, I am sure that Sunita is still with me. Even now, about 20 years after her death. Sometimes, when my family responsibilities of caring for my two children and husband get me down, I feel that I can always count on Sunita. Nothing will ever come between us.

Russell Lee: As the Spice Girls will put it, true friendships are forever!

THE GRANDFATHER CLOCK

Philip Seah, 35, magazine editor

A few years back, on a trip to Penang, I picked up a beautiful antique grandfather clock for a song. It was truly a worthy purchase. Having scraped off the years of dust and dirt, the warm, aged colours of the dark sunburst wood came through beautifully.

After cleaning it, I found that the glass surfaces were in superb condition; not a scratch on it!

Of course, I'm not a "connoisseur" of antiques, it's just that I appreciate the beauty of good workmanship. And so, the old clock was proudly installed in my home.

My wife and I decided to put it by the cabinet next to the dining table. It was very heavy, but after getting it into position, I re-checked the time and set it again, to synchronise with my watch. Strangely enough, the very second I set the time on the grandfather clock, my wristwatch stopped!

"Bong!... Bong!... Bong!"

The grandfather clock struck as it was high noon, the low mournful tones made our grey Persian tomcat curious. It was an old cat, very lazy. But it's reaction to the grandfather clock was inexplicable. It came sniffing curiously, but it wouldn't go near the clock. As the chimes ended, our cat arched its back and hissed at the grandfather clock.

"Puss, puss... tch, tch, tch... come here." My

wife called out to it but it ran off and hid. We didn't see it the rest of the day. And night.

It was a Sunday night, about nine. My daughter, Regina returned from a weekend camping trip. She had to leave for school early the next morning, so I reminded her to get a good night's sleep. In fact, I recall going to bed early myself as I had a busy day ahead.

However, at around midnight, I was still awake. I tossed and turned. With a deep, ominous sense of dread, I crept downstairs.

What I saw almost gave me a heart attack. My daughter, Regina, sat cross-legged on the floor in the hall, staring in silence at the grandfather clock.

"Regina, what are you doing?" I spluttered. My mouth was dry. My voice sounded forced and unnatural. When I saw the grin on Regina's pale bloodless face, my flesh crawled in horror.

It was her eyes. They were all pupil, no whites. Like two big black pearls, shiny with a wet shimmering light. But at quarter past midnight, when the clock struck again, she got off the floor and was her old self again.

"Regina, what are you doing, sitting out here at this time of the night? "

"I was talking to the 'uncle'."

"Uncle? What uncle?"

Without a word, she turned and looked at the antique clock in reply. And then she went up to her room. I felt the goose pimples rise on my flesh as I stood alone in the hall, silent except for the constant ticking of the clock.

Over the following days, I monitored Regina's behaviour. She was normal during the day. It was only during the night, midnight to be precise, that she appeared bewitched.

My wife and I were worried. I'm not a religious man but I was thinking of asking a bomoh or a pastor to help. But my brother-in-law, my wife's brother, Desmond, said there was no need.

"Hah... child's play!" he scoffed. "Try this simple solution — just set the clock an hour slow. But don't let your daughter know. And come the witching hour again, see what she does. She won't know, but she would've missed the real midnight hour by an hour before she goes into her little bid for attention."

I thought about it, and it sounded harmless enough. It was certainly worth a try.

And it worked! I set the grandfather clock an hour slow. So at midnight that night, it read 11pm. Which was my little girl's bedtime. And she went to bed, quiet as a lamb.

However, I didn't set the clock back to the right time. And when it struck midnight. I nearly jumped out of my skin when my wife howled.

"How dare you play about with me? How dare you!" she roared. She spoke with a man's voice! I saw that the whites of her eyes disappear. And the two black pearls in her eye sockets burned with a fury not seen in Regina's!

"You have interfered in my plans for the last time! Prepare to DIE!" She lunged at me. I fought her off as her nails went for my eyes. I turned my back and ran. She was too strong for me!

I ran out of the house while she went to sit before the grandfather clock. I peeped in through the window and watched. When the clock struck again at a quarter past midnight, she was back to her old self again.

I knew for certain there was something unnatural and unholy about the clock. Something distinctly evil but whatever it was, I just didn't want to know about it. So I didn't even try figuring it out.

"Ha ha ha… how childish! There is no such thing as ghosts!" my brother-in-law, Desmond, scoffed when I told him.

"I didn't say it was a ghost!"

"Well, what you suggest is just as ridiculous!" he said. It made what I had to do all the more easier.

I gave him the grandfather clock.

One week later, he was a changed man. He no longer thought I was childish.

Russell Lee: Time will find you out, eventually.

LOST CAMPERS

Steven Ong, 22, clerk

While we were students, some friends and I planned a "nature walk" during the holidays. After consulting a map, we decided to explore an area near Tengah River.

We started out early one morning from Lim Chu Kang Road and turned right into Ama Keng Road. Since we had enough canned food, bottled water and the necessary camping equipment packed in our haversacks, we were prepared to spend a day or two along the river.

You wouldn't know what the feeling is like to be walking in the countryside until you experience it yourselves! It's really great!

We entered Lorong Ayam Dara, which would lead us to a tributary of the Tengah River. From there, we planned to go northwards and eventually link up with Ama Keng Road.

We reached the end of Lorong Ayam Dara by mid-afternoon. We were all sweaty and welcomed a swim in the cool waters of the river. We cooked dinner and went early to sleep in our tent, since we planned to make an early start at sunrise.

When we awoke the following morning, we found ourselves in a strange place — not where we had camped! We looked around for our haversacks and were shocked to see them hanging from the high branches of nearby trees! Furthermore, we were nowhere near the river where we had a swim the previous evening!

We looked at one another, speechless! What had happened?

When we climbed the trees to get our haversacks, we found them filled with stinking, black sand! We decided to leave our haversacks and get the hell out of there. This was all too scary!

We sped through the bushes and came to a footpath which led us to a track. Breathless and terrified, we sat beside the track to rest. And, there — carefully arranged at the foot of a tree in front of us, were our camping gear and haversacks — without the stinking, black sand!

How did they get there? Who had arranged them so neatly, one on top of the other?

It was no time to seek answers. We grabbed our gear and ran along the track. After going some distance, we reached Ama Keng Road.

Safe at last! Was it all a dream? This really happened to us, Russell. My only explanation was that we had stumbled onto sacred ground and the spirits were trying to tell us to get lost. Once we left the place, they returned our belongings.

DEADLY DARLING

Russell Lee: This next story was pieced together by interviewing transvestites at Changi Village and Desker Road. It's about Cynthia. His (her?) real name is Zainal.

Cynthia was aged 29, but her beauty had never faded. She could still pass herself off as 21 or 22. She had long, slender legs, a trim figure, and a superbly enchanting oval face.

Her most precious asset was her skin. It was flawless.

Even a real woman's skin, at 29, begins to betray her age. In Cynthia's case, considering the long hours she "worked", her beautiful skin was nothing short of a miracle.

Her friends, Toni and Maria, also transvestites, but much younger, were very jealous. While they said nothing to Cynthia's face, they suspected that there was a dark secret behind her "eternal youth".

One day they followed her when she visited her "hairdresser". Cynthia took a taxi to an address in Ang Mo Kio. Sure enough, it turned out to be a bomoh's home. When they questioned the neighbours, they learned that the bomoh offered a mysterious beauty treatment.

"He sticks needles in your forehead," one of the neighbours confided, "so you can stay young forever." But what Toni and Maria didn't know was that the bomoh was Cynthia's secret lover. So when they knocked on his door asking for the "needles that keep you young", the bomoh suspected that the two were Cynthia's rivals for Cynthia had confided to the bomoh of the raging jealousy of her "friends" and how she was bullied without mercy.

Inviting them inside, the bomoh decided he would give them a beauty treatment of a different kind!

He told Toni and Maria to lie on two mattresses on the floor. He produced his needles, and soaked them in a special magic fluid. What the two hapless transvestites didn't know was that the fluid contained rat poison.

After the "treatment", which cost $200, Toni and Maria returned to their squalid flat in Bendemeer Road. Within hours they became ill, their faces erupting in hideous boils and scars.

Disfigured badly, the two transvestites flew

into a rage. A few nights later, when at last they were able to stagger from their flat, they confronted Cynthia in Desker Road. Accusing her of trying to kill them, they attacked her with knives.

But the bomoh's magic worked against them once more. A police patrol car pulled up, and the screaming duo were hauled off to prison. According to our sources, Toni hanged herself in her cell while Maria eventually fled to Malaysia where she later went mad.

Cynthia had been slashed badly in the attack, but after consulting her "hairdresser" bomoh, her scars vanished overnight.

Today, she is still as beautiful as ever. Some say she is now well over 35, but looks even younger than before.

Russell Lee: Cynthia may be a darling but she's deadly as well.

A SPECIAL STORY

Russell Lee: Remember Frankie Fearless from Book 9? He asked for another assignment after the Tok Tai Lalat story and this next piece is the result.

PHARAOH'S BOOKMARK

Frankie Fearless, 28, ghost writer

My elder sister, an air stewardess with Singapore Airlines, received a free return ticket to London early this year. As I was her beloved baby brother, she gave it to me.

I vowed to really enjoy myself during the two-week trip. The list of "can-you-get-me's" from friends was long: CDs, videos, books, the usual stuff.

One item, however, stood out. A bookmark. To be exact, Pharaoh's Bookmark. My girlfriend, Sasha, who's into the supernatural seemed intent on getting it. She had done research on it and even knew the bookshop to get it from.

A Roman Catholic by birth, Sasha grew up in a conservative family. But Sasha soon became rebellious, determined to chart her own lifestyle. Sasha was into "Goth". She was quite tall, very skinny and pale, and, looked cool in black.

Sasha, however, had an unhealthy interest in the occult which I suspected was the reason she sought for the bookmark. I was right for Sasha later explained to me the occult roots of the bookmark. It originated from the time of the Pharaohs, thousands of years ago. It was supposed to have magical qualities that could transport you into a thousand different worlds. Only two such bookmarks were known to exist.

When Sasha saw the funny look on my face, she blurted, "Just get the bookmark, lah! Why you ask so many questions?"

In London, I had a bit of trouble locating the bookshop. It was tucked away in a corner.

A tall, old lady welcomed me into the shop. In her late 60's, she was stylish and elegant. She wore a long black dress with lacy sleeves and was

116

draped with gypsy scarves. Her straight hair hung down to her waist, and her raven-black eyes stared above her wide crimson lips, like her long fingernails, painted a deep blood red.

"Where are you from, young man?"

"Sing… Singapore," I mumbled. "I'm looking for Pharaoh's Bookmark."

"Why do you seek Pharaoh's Bookmark?" she asked. "Are you a 'seeker'?"

"Same to you!" I said, thinking that she had said "sucker". It was her accent, it was difficult to understand her.

The gypsy woman frowned and stared at me as if trying to make up her mind about me. Then she shrugged and handed me a card.

"Whatever," she said, "this is my card, I run another bookshop in Notting Hill. This will help you."

"Thanks!" I said, happy at this breakthrough.

I looked at the card. "The Equinox Bookstore", it said in bold Gothic typeface. The design was intricate and old world; I was quite sure I would find the bookmark there. By now, I began to sense that "Pharaoh's Bookmark" was something special. Perhaps I would get it for myself!

I reached the bookshop in the evening. From the streets, I saw the pale gold lights of the bookstore glowing in the gathering purple dusk. It was old and rundown, but it looked cosy and warm. "The Equinox", said the sign above the door.

The air inside the shop was thick and fragrant with burning incense. The shelves were stacked with all sorts of books. An old Mediterranean looking gentleman stood behind the counter.

"Excuse me, I want to buy Pharaoh's Bookmark," I said, taking a shot in the dark.

The response was encouraging: "What do you know about the bookmark?"

"Do you have it?"

He looked me in the eye. "It's not for sale."

I told him that I was a "seeker", hoping that the mention of the word would help. It did make him shift about nervously.

"I've been seeking for nine long years. I will give you anything," I said, lying blatantly.

"My name is Abdul Waheed," the man said, in a kinder tone. "I understand. I'll help you. But as I said, Pharaoh's Bookmark is not for sale."

Saying thus, he held up a strip of dark reddish brown leather. It was tasselled and it's surface had Egyptian hieroglyphics carved into it.

"This," he said, "is Pharaoh's Bookmark."

I thanked him as I pulled out my credit card.

He put up his hand, stopping me. "As I said, it's not for sale. But are you sure you want it?"

I couldn't believe my ears. "Yes!" I said.

I was quite sure that I'd keep the mysterious bookmark for myself. Why was this thing so precious?

On the flight back to Singapore, I started reading "Almanac of the Uncanny," a book about the history of supernatural happenings. Without thinking, I slipped Pharaoh's Bookmark in between the pages as I drifted to sleep.

And the most incredible thing happened... I dreamed I was actually experiencing the events described in the book. It so happened that the bookmark was facing page 11, where there was a description of Pharaoh Khufu. The Great Pyramid was built for him in Giza around the 26 century BC. I also learned that the treasures interred with the Pharaoh were taken by robbers. I saw that one of the stolen items was the bookmark!

I awoke. The dream was so vivid, I felt that I was inside the Great Pyramid! I saw the king's burial chamber and the elaborate passageways.

It felt good! But surely this must be some freakish coincidence? That night, as the plane took off after stopping in Bahrain, I slipped Pharaoh's Bookmark in a music mag I got in Soho for a friend and... I was performing in a rock concert! I woke up before things got really out of hand. The flight steward was shaking me hard, thinking that I was in a fit or drunk.

I tested it again and it worked... like a dream! I found that I could transport myself into any world, merely by slipping the bookmark between the pages of a book or magazine.

Over the next few days, I had a marvellous time. I could actually live the life of anything I chose! From Gu Long sword-fighting novels, to romances like the Great Gatsby.

Days passed. I hardly ever went out. In fact, I rarely even left my room. And then, one day I had a disgruntled visitor.

"What the hell's happened to you? How come you didn't call me all this time?" It was Sasha and she was in a terrible mood. Not only did I not call, I had missed her birthday as well!

"What a creep you are, Frankie! And I thought you were a nice guy! I bet you didn't even look for Pharaoh's Bookmark!"

I told her what had happened... everything. I handed over the bookmark to her.

A week went by, and I was starting to worry. Not just about Sasha, but about my precious magical bookmark as well.

When I went over to Sasha's place, my heart sank. I could sense the air of tragedy the minute I stepped inside. Her family was there, and they looked distraught. I pulled Sasha to a corner.

"What happened? Did you try it?"

"No, I didn't... but my father did... my poor father."

She led me, at this point, to her father's room... and I saw.

Indeed, he had used the bookmark... There he lay on his bed — muttering and drooling, cackling insanely. You could see it in his eyes — his mind was gone. His spirit was shattered, his soul destroyed.

And there, on the bedside table, lay Pharaoh's Bookmark... in the book which destroyed him.

And I saw the title of that terrible book.

It was Dante's "Inferno".

Russell Lee: If only Sasha's dad had stuck to safe books like The Solid Singapore-Malaysia Joke Book!

PART VI

RUSSELL LEE INTERVIEWS EILEEN WEE

Russell Lee: This is a new section that we have started. Occasionally, I will interview well-known and interesting public personalities for their experiences with the supernatural. Our first interview is with Eileen Wee, famous for her part in the money-spinning films, "Money No Enough!", "Army Daze" and "Mee Pok Man".

CALL FROM HELL

Eileen Wee, 24, actress

Russell Lee: You know, you look better in real life than on TV or the movies.

Eileen Wee: Thank you, you're very kind.

Russell Lee: I like the Shivers episode with you and Michelle Goh in it. You are prettier than Michelle, I think.

Eileen Wee: I think so too... ha ha ha. Why are you wearing a hood?

Russell Lee: It's part of my job. Anyway, I look like a beast without my mask.

Eileen Wee: Me beauty, you beast. Beauty and the beast... ha ha.

Russell Lee: So vain. Please tell me your story. It sounds like it's going to be a funny one.

Eileen Wee: My story is anything but funny. I get the creeps even thinking about the incident. My family was on holiday in Penang and we booked into an old but charming hotel. The rooms were small and my sister and I shared a room while my parents took another.

Soon after checking in, I went shopping with my sis even though I was quite tired. After four hours of trudging through the many spanking new shopping malls of the island, I bought myself a pair of high-heels that were made in Thailand! My sister thought I was crazy.

However the hot, humid weather and the travelling took its toll on me and after a shower I was so tired that I skipped dinner and fell into bed. At about midnight, the phone rang. I reluctantly picked up the phone because I knew my sis slept soundly and not even a bomb blast would wake her up.

"Get out of here!" a creepy voice said. I thought that it was someone playing a joke.

"Sorry, wrong number," I said and hung up.

The phone rang again. This time, I had a sinking feeling in my gut. It was the same hoarse voice. It was angry.

"You better get out of my room!"

I was tired, hungry and now, very, very angry. "Go to HELL! If you call one more time, I'm calling the police!" I slammed the receiver down. I looked over at my sister, sleeping like a pig and muttered, "What the heck! After all that and she's still sleeping!"

The phone rang again. I stared at it. It kept on ringing.

An unseen power drew me to the phone inspite of myself. As soon as I picked up the phone, the voice hurled abuse at me, swearing and cursing. But I wasn't listening to the voice. My attention was on the background sounds. People were screaming and wailing. There was splashing and a crackling sound, like a forest fire. It was like there were so many people in there, so many people and so much anguish. It sounded like… HELL. My shaking hand let the phone fall to the floor.

I woke my sister up and dragged her down to see the duty manager. My sister didn't believe a word I said. But she was surprised when the manager said to her, "No, your sister is telling the truth. A man committed suicide in that room."

I didn't really appreciate his honesty. We should never have been given that room in the first place. I was only placated when they upgraded us into a much better room. I called my parents and told them of the room change.

I was about to doze off when the phone rang. My parents, I assumed.

"Get out! Get out of my hotel…" This time the background sounds were so clear.

My sister and I checked out of the hotel immediately. We refused to pay the bill.

Russell Lee: Maybe you were trying to get off without paying?

Eileen Wee: What? No way! Talking about money, am I being paid for this interview or not?

Russell Lee: Money no enough, is it?

Eileen Wee: Go to hell, lah!

Russell Lee: Yes, yes… I guess it's time for me to go home. I'll call you later…

PART VII

THE SINISTER SISTER

Beverly Tsao, 27, unemployed

About three years ago, my brother was rushed to a Singapore hospital for an emergency operation. It's a very famous hospital and I'm sure you would know it. But I can't tell you its name for reasons which will become clear.

The surgeons saved my brother's life. I went to see him soon after the operation. He was very cheerful for a while, making a perfect recovery, then suddenly he developed a fever and lapsed into a coma. The doctors were puzzled and were trying to find out what had gone wrong.

We kept a vigil by his bed. My elderly parents sat there praying all day. At night, after work, I took over, sitting there, watching his pale face and faint breathing.

One night I needed to go to the ladies. It was very late and the corridors were dark. As I was returning to his bedside, I heard a strange sobbing sound.

Suddenly a woman in a white uniform came hurrying from his room. She was carrying a tray with a white cloth over it. Her face was torn with agony. Thinking my brother had taken a sudden turn, I called to her.

"Sister, is something wrong?"

She looked at me with haunted eyes. My guts froze over. Her crisp, starched uniform had an eerie glow about it. She held up the tray and lifted the cloth.

I gasped. There, on the metal tray, was a human heart, red with wet blood. It was still pumping. I couldn't believe it. Was I dreaming?

They'd removed my brother's heart!

I choked. I pushed past the sister, racing to his room. I flung open the door. He was still sleeping, only the most peaceful look had settled onto his face.

My whole body was shaking with fear. I had to talk to the sister, but she'd vanished. I looked everywhere, my eyes wide with panic.

A warder caught me by the arm and asked me what the matter was.

"The sister," I blurted, "she had my brother's heart…"

He looked alarmed. He drew me into the shadows, making sure no one could hear him.

"You saw the old sister," he explained. "She worked here in this ward for many years."

"She still does!" I shouted. "I've just seen her!"

He shook his head sadly. "No. She died some time ago. The man she loved, a doctor, broke her heart. She killed herself by taking drugs from the hospital pharmacy."

I was quaking. "No, you don't understand! I just saw her…"

"There are things we can't explain," he told me, placing an arm around my shoulder. "Believe me, she is very dead but she comes back to visit, as though she was still on duty. She still tries to help patients who are ill to pull through by carrying away all the evil spirits."

Just after that, my brother made a full recovery. The doctors said it was a miracle, but I know the truth. I believe it was the sister's magic. She helped him pull through. Her life was over, but not her life's work.

Russell Lee: Although an illness can be attributed to evil spirits, I would caution against blaming spirits for every sickness. I know of cult groups that do this. They even refuse medical attention, preferring to "pray" for a cure. Many die needlessly.

THE KATONG TAPPER

Zak Ismail, 18, student

Many years ago, the East Coast Road in Katong was lined with rubber plantations. Some of the old-timers can still remember them in the area near Holy Family Church.

An old Indian man told me this story. He was sitting in his stall late one night when he met his great-grandfather.

My friends and I didn't believe him, until he reached under the counter and held up a bag of old Indian coins.

"My great-grandfather came back from the dead, to bring me these…"

Great-grandfather Ravi had been brought to Singapore by the British. He had worked as a labourer, constructing the old colonial buildings by the Singapore River. Eventually, Ravi had saved enough money to send for his bride.

Together they worked for a plantation owner in Katong. They rose every morning before sunrise, tapping the trees in the estate for their precious rubber. As the years went by, their family grew up and went off to live in other parts of the island. Ravi, his back stooped by years of grinding toil, dreamed of seeing India once more before his death.

But the old man's wish was not to be.

His wife died of a snake bite and he never quite recovered from the sudden loss. All alone, he set sail for India but the ship was lost at sea. Some say it sank in a storm. Others said it was attacked by pirates who slaughtered all those aboard.

Ravi became nothing more than a memory.

And so, one night, about six years ago, the stallholder was closing up for the night, wondering how he would settle all his debts, when he heard a car slam on its brakes in East Coast Road. It had narrowly missed an elderly pedestrian.

The stallholder helped the man to his feet.

"You were lucky," he said to the skeletal gentleman.

"Where are the trees?" a weary voice had asked. "Where is my family?"

The stallholder thought the gentleman had lost his mind. He poured him some of the remaining tea from his flask.

"Thank you, Kumar," the mysterious gentleman said.

The stallholder gasped. "How do you know my name?"

"You're my great-grandson. I'm Ravi, I've

come back to help you."

Ravi's ship, it turned out, had indeed been lost at sea, swamped by a giant wave. But the old man didn't drown. The currents had carried him to a mystical island where he lived forever with other sea ghosts.

Hearing that one of his family members needed money, he had been permitted to visit Singapore for one night. He had stepped ashore on the reclaimed land, where once only the sea had been. He walked inland, searching for old landmarks, but found none. Tall HDB blocks and shopping complexes had replaced the old familiar landscape.

His beloved rubber trees had vanished. He was so disoriented that he didn't see the car rushing towards him.

"Here is the money I have saved for you," Ravi said, handing over the bag of coins.

Then he had walked away into the night.

The stallholder showed us the blackened coins.

"I am sure they are worth a fortune to a coin collector or a museum," he said. "But how can I part with my great-grandfather's treasure?"

We agreed with him. And we all hoped that Ravi had made it safely back to that island and the other sea ghosts.

DAUGHTER OF SATAN

Selena Tan, 39, manager

My four elder brothers are all soccer fanatics so I grew up loving the sport. Although my favourite team is Manchester United, I enjoy watching the Singapore side playing as well. I followed the Malaysia Cup competition with keen interest, hardly ever missing a game.

One Saturday, some years ago, after watching an exciting match against arch-rivals Selangor at the National Stadium, I was walking along Old Airport Road on my way home. There were many others walking in the same direction. Everybody was celebrating and chattering loudly because Singapore had won the close contest.

When I reached the Mountbatten Road junction, I saw a woman standing beside the road. She was looking directly at me. It was weird because I didn't recognise her at all.

As I approached her, she moved quickly and stood right in front of me, blocking my way. I stepped aside and as I walked past her, I detected a strong scent of flowers.

"Prostitute," I thought.

I carried on walking, along with the crowd and when I looked over my shoulder, I saw she was close behind me, grinning.

I had to stop at the next junction for the lights and deliberately stood close to other people. By now, the determination of the woman unsettled me. Even the crowds didn't put her off.

The next thing I knew, she was standing right beside me! I couldn't get a look at her face because she was shielding it with the palm of her left hand and I noticed her fingernails — they were long and pointed!

As the pedestrian lights turned to green, I ran across the road and started to walk quickly towards the food centre nearby. I was relieved when I turned the corner — I was finally rid of her. I ran to a public phone to call my brothers. It would be really nice if they could come and meet me. I fidgeted while waiting for a woman to finish her call. She was taking so long. When she finally finished, I rushed forward, not waiting for her to get out of the booth.

She turned around and — IT WAS HER!

I ran so fast that I was breathless by the time I reached the lift, relieved. I said some prayers as I got into the lift with two others. Good. At least there was some company. At the sixth floor, one of them got off. And as the lift started again, the remaining person turned around — it was the damn woman again! It was then that I got a good look at her face. Her skin was grey and scaly. Her lips were cracked and she had yellow eyes!

I loudly recited some prayers. The lift came to a halt on the third floor. There was no time to lose. I had to do something.

"Daughter of Satan, GO AWAY!" I shouted.

I spat into her face and she covered it with her hands and screamed — a horrible, high-pitched scream!

And then, she vanished. Just like that.

To this day, I don't know why she followed me. I've never seen her again. Since that encounter, I have never visited the National Stadium. I watch S-League football now.

Russell Lee: Let's hope the "kelong" in Singapore football vanishes away just as easily as your "daughter of Satan".

CASPER

Dudley Yeo, 29, schoolteacher

I have this story to tell which happened to me two years ago. Then, all I wanted to do was to forget the horror. But Russell, your True Singapore Ghost Stories prompted me to write this.

After graduating from the Institute of Education, I was posted to an all-boys school, which I shall not name.

Since I was new I was given a lot of tough assignments which nobody else wanted. One of which was to take a group of lower secondary boys to St John's Island.

There were about 30 students and I was the only adult. I didn't relish the responsibility, I can tell you that. I was very glad when a freak thunderstorm broke out when we all arrived at the island, cancelling all planned activities like swimming and hiking.

And so we stayed indoors at the campsite. It was an old building, quite nice actually, surrounded by tall swaying palms. I think it used to be some sort of military hospital built by the British.

None of that mattered to the kids though, who rattled the very foundations of the building with the noise they made. The wide spaces of the place, with it's high ceilings and empty rooms, seemed to accommodate the bedlam of the boisterous brats.

This is it, I could relax. This way, there was less chance of anyone getting hurt. Why, the evening could even turn out to be enjoyable, I thought.

It had stopped raining, however, and the night was hot and humid. All the "quaint" features about the place now lost its charm.

There was no air-conditioning. And the ceiling fans merely rattled as they rotated, they didn't cool you. The electric lights were dirty and dim, making everything dismal and weary. Time seemed to stand still as I fell into a fitful rest.

Suddenly, I heard a scream coming from one of the rooms. I tried to locate my slippers in the dark but couldn't, I must have kicked them under the bed accidentally. And so I ran over barefooted.

"Ghost! Ghost!" shouted Yong Xing, a boy from class 2B. Although the others in the room didn't say anything, they looked like they had actually seen a ghost.

"It's just a bad dream," I said to the big group that had, by then, gathered. "Go back to sleep, all of you."

"It's not a bad dream, sir... I saw it. I really, really saw it!" Yong Xing said. And before I could stop him, he was telling everyone about it.

"I saw something standing at the window! I saw! There's something there!"

Before Yong Xing could finish, the others started screaming. The hysteria was spreading.

"Quiet… shut up… SHUT UP!" I tried to take charge.

"Listen," I said, addressing them, "we all know Yong Xing is a real practical joker! He's only playing a trick on you. Don't tell me you all are scared?" I knew that no-one would admit to being scared.

"And you," I said to Yong Xing, "I know you read a lot of Russell Lee books, but don't make me fed up, okay?"

Some laughed, unconvincingly. I looked at Yong Xing. What I saw unnerved me — the kid was serious. He was scared, really scared.

Before I could get into bed again, I had to run to the room where the other boys were sleeping. More than one voice was screaming this time.

"Not again!" I thought. This time I saw… chaos.

The lone light bulb, yellow and dim, hanging from the ceiling swung violently round and round. Creating a giddy effect with it's circular motion, it made the room spin…

In that scene of confusion, I saw the belongings of the boys in that room; clothes, shoes, bags, toothbrushes violently scattered about the room. Mattresses were off the beds. It was a battlefield.

All around me were the ashen faces of the boys, trembling a little now... in fear. A deep, real fear on the edge of stark raving terror. Jacob, the class monitor, started to talk...

"We were coming back from Yong Xing's room, sir. We heard a commotion and when I switched on the lights, I saw... standing in the centre of the room, throwing everything around... I suh-suh... saw... saw..." He was shaking uncontrollably.

Rudy, the Indonesian lad, continued, "It was a ghost, sir! A real GHOST!"

And that set the rest of them off.

"A ghost... a ghost!"

"I want to go home... I want to go home..."

I had a case of mass hysteria on my hands. To tell you the truth, I was feeling scared myself.

I tried to calm things down. "Look, Rudy, how do you know it was a ghost? And if it really was a ghost, what was it like? Where is it now?"

Rudy's face turned pale as he turned to look up at the light bulb, still swinging round and round. We all followed his gaze and looked at the light bulb dangling from the ceiling, suddenly coming to a dead stop.

"When Jeremy switched on the lights, I saw it...," Rudy said. "It... it... like a baby... but big... HUGE! A huge black baby... it had an even bigger head, a big, big head but with a man's face. The eyes were shining. When it saw us come in, it tried to go out through the window. When it couldn't, it jumped on the light bulb."

I saw now how the window in the room was fitted with iron grilles. What the boy said made

136

sense.

"That means," I said, "that it's still here in the room, now." I stared at the empty space around the light bulb and saw an unmistakable jolt, a twitch of movement.

The fear in the room was thick and oppressing. The smell of urine was distinct; someone had wet himself. There was a low, weeping noise from some of the boys, murmuring prayers or simply crying in helpless despair. I had to do something...

"Oh! So there you are Mr Ghost! I almost didn't see you... can you come down a minute so we can talk?" I said, trying to assume my usual casual classroom manner. To dispel the fear with something familiar.

"Ah," I said, addressing the blank space beside me as if the ghost was standing there.

"Well, well, Mr Ghost, how are you? Okay? Good, good."

I went on with the game. Some of the kids giggled nervously.

"I hope you don't mind me asking, but... what do you want? You're scaring everyone, you know?"

I spoke as if the ghost and I were having a casual chat. It worked — the tension dispersed!

"What's your name?... Casper? Well, you must be a friendly ghost then, ha, ha. What's that you say? Is it? You want a drink of water? That's all? You sure you don't want a Pepsi or something else instead? No? Okay."

Saying this, I picked up a plastic water bottle from the floor and poured the "ghost" a plastic cupful, setting the cup on the table beside myself and my invisible guest.

I could feel the paralysing spell lift as I carried on chatting to the space beside me.

"How are things in general, okay? Good, hah? What's that you say? You're busy? After finishing this drink, you got to go? Well, don't let me delay you... but take your time... finish your drink first then go..." I prattled on.

Some of the kids were laughing at this point. I thought I had the situation well under control.

Until...

We all saw, right before our very eyes... the little plastic cup float eerily into the air, tilting itself, emptying its liquid contents. You could see the water being poured out... *but not a drop of it touched the floor!*

After it was completely drained, it was set back down on the table. I felt a gust of cold air rush by me... heading for the door.

I was very badly shaken after that but strangely enough, the kids weren't! They all went to bed and slept easily while I stayed up, chain-smoking till dawn.

I asked a few of them the next day, how on earth they could sleep so easily?

I got the same response. You see, they went along with every little gesture when I played host to the ghost. They believed my every word. And they took the word of our "guest" as well — to leave them alone after he had his drink of water.

He was, after all, Casper, a friendly ghost.

Russell Lee: My team of writers followed a lead provided by a radio deejay for the next story. I cannot vouch for its truth because the deejay says that it's only an unconfirmed rumour. Judge for yourself.

THE SINGING SPIRIT OF CALDECOTT HILL

Today if you go to Caldecott Hill, the massive studios and satellite dishes of the television complex will dominate your view. But many years ago, in the days when it was called RTS (Radio and Television Singapore), the buildings were smaller and simpler.

Instead of all the famous stars we have today, the performers were paid a lot less. Many of them have been forgotten now, lost to our memory, even to our grandparents' memory.

But there was one tragic case which came to light when the new TV studios were being built. When the workmen were excavating the hillside, in a little patch of jungle, the skeleton of a young woman was unearthed. The story never reached the media but our reliable sources have unearthed the true story behind The Singing Spirit of Caldecott Hill.

It all began in the 1960's, when television first arrived in Singapore. Before TV, there was only the radio. And in those days, one of the most popular radio artistes was a singer we shall call by the name of Jenny Ng.

Jenny sang Mandarin songs. For years she had been the toast of Singapore. Her name was a household word. Her voice was pure and young,

139

despite the fact she was reaching her 42nd birthday. With television just around the corner, Jenny feared that her age would mean the end of her career.

"No, you are still beautiful," her friends assured her. "Your fans will never desert you!"

But inside, Jenny became tormented with doubt and jealousy. Every morning, when she faced her mirror, she could see the tell-tale lines and wrinkles of middle age. Her breasts were no longer firm. Her figure was losing its youth. It was only a matter of time before the newfangled TV cameras told the truth about her!

She feared that one day her fans would laugh at her and call her old. But, being a seasoned performer, she kept her fears under control and presented her usual smiling, confident personality to the rest of the world.

One afternoon though, her world came crashing down around her. She had just finished recording some songs with the RTS band. All the musicians applauded her. She was the star!

Just at that moment, one of the studio managers brought a shy young woman to the microphone. He introduced her to Jenny.

"Jenny, this is Miss Gloria de Souza. She is our latest discovery."

Jenny looked at the most beautiful girl she had ever seen. No older than 18, the Eurasian had olive skin which glowed, large eyes full of expression, and when she began to sing with the band, her notes were so true, so pure that Jenny knew she had met her nemesis!

Gloria de Souza had a better face, a better body, and damn, damn, damn… a better voice!

The older singer politely applauded with everyone else when the girl had finished her song. Then, stepping forward, she took Gloria by the arm.

"My darling, you are going to be a wonderful star. Please allow me to help you with a few tips about your singing."

Gloria innocently met her gaze. "Oh, Miss Ng, would you do that for me? It would be such an honour…"

Little did Gloria realise she was playing into the older woman's trap.

So Jenny Ng "befriended" the young singer. She took her to the canteen, told her all about the studio, promised to help her whenever she could.

Gloria couldn't believe how lucky she was! Here was Jenny Ng, the singing star of Singapore for generations, offering to guide her rise to stardom. And when Jenny suggested they take a little walk around the grounds, Gloria agreed.

She was never seen again!

According to our sources, Jenny walked Gloria across the main compound, past all the busy studio buildings, and out towards the grove of jungle by the fence. It was early evening, and no one else was in that vicinity.

Hidden by the trees, with no witnesses, Jenny picked up a rock. Without warning, she smashed it down on the younger woman's skull. Again and again she rained blows down on the poor girl's head. If Gloria screamed, who would have heard her? Everyone was inside the studios, all outside sounds drowned out by the noise of a broadcasting complex going to air.

The ground was wet and soft. Jenny picked up a workman's spade and dug a shallow grave, Gloria's dead body was soon covered by dirt and leaves.

The next day, the studio managers confronted the staff anxiously. Everybody was looking for Gloria. Jenny said she had seen Gloria leave the station with a young man driving a green car. The police were informed, but their search was fruitless.

Gloria's parents offered a reward. No one ever stepped forward to claim it.

As the weeks passed, Gloria de Souza was forgotten.

Jenny's career, meanwhile, progressed to even greater heights. She was the most popular TV singer of all, and her fans adored her.

But the secret guilt was tearing Jenny apart. She had taken another human life, and there would be a price to pay.

The price?

Her own life. A year on, Jenny's car rolled over an embankment and her badly disfigured face was barely recognised.

Jenny Ng was as dead as Gloria de Souza.

Except for one interesting fact: Gloria's voice can still be heard. According to some of the musicians who were at that recording session with Jenny and Gloria, they can still hear Gloria's sweet voice echoing through the corridor of the new studio complex. It is a voice they swear that they will never forget.

A SPECIAL STORY

THE WHITE GHOSTS OF CHANGI

James Wheatley, 53, advertising executive

"No one has ever lived in that house," the real estate salesman told me. "Well, not for more than one night."

I looked at the detached bungalow. It was the end house in a row of stylish homes. But despite the fact it was only five years old, it bore all the signs of decay. Black stains had disfigured its walls. The windows were empty black sockets, like sightless eyes, devoid of curtains. Tangled grass choked the garden.

"It's half the price of the other houses," said the salesman. "But better not buy! It'll not make you happy. Feng shui no good."

Of course I bought it! Who wouldn't? It was a fantastic investment. Before my wife and I shifted, the contractors repainted it and cleaned up the mess. We moved in on a Monday afternoon. It was perfect. One of the neighbours called by to wish us "good luck", which we felt was rather strange.

That night, my tired wife went to bed early. I sat up watching television. It must have been 10 o'clock when I began to feel chilly. My skin was crawling, my eyes burned, and a pain stabbed into the pit of my stomach. I leapt up and ran to the back door. Outside, everything appeared to be normal. Until the moon drifted behind a cloud and I caught a movement in the shadows by the back fence.

Someone was there. Someone covered in rags. But no, they weren't the rags of a beggar. It was the remains of an army uniform, all stained with blood.

Another shape appeared, stooped and groaning, also clad in a tattered uniform. They were carrying spades and started to dig two holes in my garden.

I uttered a feeble cry and slammed the door. I raced upstairs, bathed in sweat. My wife was sleeping peacefully. I lit some incense and climbed into bed beside her. Mercifully, I was soon asleep.

The next morning, in the bright sunlight, everything was tranquil. I stared out at the garden, but there were no signs of the ground having been disturbed.

I didn't tell my wife what I had seen. I dropped her off at a bus stop. Then instead of driving to my office in Loyang, I headed for the nearest temple. I explained to a monk what I had seen the night before. He nodded sympathetically.

"Your house is not far from Changi Prison," he explained. "During the Japanese Occupation, thousands of British prisoners were tortured and killed there. Sometimes the Japanese made them dig their own graves in the jungle before putting a bayonet into their stomachs."

I knew what I had to do! I hurried to Changi Village. In one of the little shops full of odd merchandise I found two British flags, small ones that schoolchildren might wave. They were left over from the days when British troops were stationed in the area.

That evening, while my wife was bathing, I crept out into the garden and planted them in the soil. Then I waited.

Ten o'clock came and went. Eleven o'clock, and the garden was still peaceful. At midnight, I went to bed, secure in the knowledge that I had given the two British soldiers the dignity of marking their graves with their country's flag.

I told the monk what I had done and he said I was very wise. Then he took me aside and told me about other "strange" incidents in Changi.

A British major, whose wife and two daughters were tortured, raped and killed, can still be heard weeping for his family. Sometimes, if you wait at the junction of Loyang Avenue and Changi Village Road, you can see this British family walking down Changi Village Road. You have to wait till about four in the morning to "see" the family. It's said that the family used to walk that way during happier times.

And, recently, on Changi Beach, a Japanese tourist almost drowned. The hapless tourist had stepped into shallow water. Suddenly, the poor fellow was pulled down into the sea. He screamed for help and onlookers quickly rushed to his aid. After his rescue, he said that hundreds of "hands" had been tearing at his body. In fact, his rescuers discovered claw marks on his legs and stomach.

The monk explained: "It was at Changi Beach that the Japanese Army machine-gunned innocent Chinese civilians. So when that Japanese tourist went swimming, the spirits of the dead Chinese wanted their revenge."

I also learned that guards and prisoners at Changi Prison often hear pitiful screams and gunshots late at night or early in the morning.

Russell, perhaps your readers have other stories to tell about ghosts in the Changi district?

PART VIII

Russell Lee: The entries are getting better all the time. The best stories, however, are the ones with a personal touch. Some didn't include addresses. So if you want to claim your prize, please write in. We'll have to confirm your identity. The winners here receive $50 each. Other winners are listed on page 10.

The Angsana Russell Lee Prize Winners

ALL BOTTLED UP

Shahul Hameed, 12, student

Our new Indonesian maid was a very shy sort and went about her chores without much fuss. Although we thought her to be honest and sincere, things in my two-storey, semi-detached home began to disappear soon after her arrival.

My father's watch, money and mother's jewellery vanished without even a trace. I was really sore when one day my new 120-dollar Lotto soccer boots went missing. I had saved for a long time to buy that pair. We were all puzzled but still didn't suspect that the new maid had anything to do with it.

One night, my younger brother, who's really quite cheeky, peeped into the maid's room because he heard some chants coming from her room. The door was left ajar.

What he saw made his blood freeze. The maid

was lying prostrate before a black bottle and there were joss-sticks and herbs lying about. As my kid brother was watching, an ugly dwarf came wriggling out of the bottle! Its naked body was covered with slime and hair and it grinned an evil, threatening smile.

"Grrrr... grrr" it growled. It was a toyol; my brother had read enough ghost stories to know that.

The maid suddenly chanted even louder.

My brother let out a gasp and immediately the maid looked over and saw my brother. The toyol knew that there was an unwelcome intrusion and scampered back into the safety of the bottle.

My brother reported what he saw to my dad who called in a bomoh the next day. No wonder objects were disappearing. It was the naughty spirit that was responsible.

The bomoh said prayers and with the use of some "jampi-jampi" or holy water, he finally pronounced the place "clean". Needless to say, the maid was sacked.

Despite the advice of the bomoh and the strong protests of mum, my father wanted the black, opaque bottle for himself.

I know that he keeps it in the cupboard in his bedroom.

Russell Lee: Hmm... is there going to be a sequel to this story?

THE "HARIMAU" SPIRIT

Kassim Sultan, 17, student

During the school holidays last year, I worked as a night watchman in a Woodlands warehouse. After the interview in the company's office in town, I was directed to the warehouse. Only a private mini-bus service serviced the area in half-hour intervals.

On the first night, I missed the bus. I telephoned the warehouse and apologised for being late. The person I spoke to seemed understanding. He sounded like an old man and had a kind, gentle, soft-spoken voice. He was the permanent night watchman and I was to be his assistant.

He gave me directions. It was only around seven but it was already dark. I was about to give up when I saw the bridge and monsoon canal the old man had described.

The narrow wooden bridge was old and shaky. As I stepped on it, there was a flash of lightning and thunder. I walked faster. As the darkness enclosed me, I heard a soft purring sound and the leaves rustle. Two dark green eyes were staring at me. Cat eyes — except that they belonged to an animal much bigger than a cat.

My heart thumped. Laughing nervously, I told myself not to be silly! How could it be? Maybe it was another cat that had escaped from the zoo!

The rain started to pour and my head swirled as I smelled a thick, musky smell of animal blood!

I heard the sound again, only this time it was

a loud roar! I turned back and there it was — a pair of bright yellow feline eyes… glowing in the dark, the downpour doing nothing to diminish its intensity.

My legs turned to rubber but I still managed to run, screaming for help. I ran to the warehouse. There was movement in the foliage, as though the "animal" was tailing me.

It was a huge place, a little rundown and dimly lit. There was a tall perimeter fence around it, topped with tangles of thick barbed wire. More suitable for an army camp or prison than a warehouse. Perhaps there was valuable stuff in there.

There was a guardroom at the gates. The lights were all off but the door was unlocked. I was told to report to the guardroom so I let myself in.

It was lit by a flickering light bulb. It felt warm and cosy as the rain fell heavily. An old man wearing a raincoat and carrying a torchlight came in. He slammed the torchlight on the table, and took off his raincoat, violently flicking it, shaking off the wet droplets.

"Sial!" he cursed. I recognised his voice. He was the man I spoke to on the phone. But he didn't seem like the same person at all.

"Youngsters nowadays all useless! Stupid, lazy, ignorant!" he said. But I didn't take the words personally.

"Do you know what to do or not? Hah? Come late… everything I got to show you!"

He was starting to get on my nerves. He explained I had to make the rounds every two hours, and sign the security books at every checkpoint.

"Now you nothing to do right? Come!" he said. I followed. But my patience ran out when he gave me a mop and asked me to clean the toilet!

"Go to hell!" I snapped.

He spluttered in fury and his eyes were popping out of their sockets. The old guy freaked out and threw a fit, his body twitching and shaking!

"Pak Chik! Pak... are you okay? I'm sorry, okay?" Suddenly, his eyes shot open and stared at me. His eyes had changed... they were glowing now, a bright yellow light... cat eyes! And he opened his mouth and roared like a tiger.

I fell backwards... away from this madness. I backed into the toilet, kicking the door shut as he picked himself up and lunged at me. He slammed his whole body at the door and began clawing it.

I don't know how long I remained in the loo but when the rain stopped, I was still shaking. It had become quiet but I wasn't eager to go out. Eventually, I opened the door.

"Hello."

The old man's gentle voice startled me. He was all right. This was the Pak Chik that I had spoken to on the phone.

He had been possessed, he explained, by the "harimau spirit", the tiger spirit.

I called the office the next day and quit.

"Why?" the clerk asked.

I told her the story. There was a long pause.

"But there is no old man there," she said. No one's supposed to be there! Only you!"

With a shaking hand, I hung up.

COOL POOL

Sheryl Wong, 26, model

My boyfriend and I moved into a condominium apartment about a month ago. We were pretty excited. This place had everything: squash, tennis, sauna, gym. But best of all, it had a cool swimming pool. I love to swim. Besides, it keeps me in good shape. And that's important for a model.

Of course, I tried out the pool as soon as I could. I decided to do a couple of laps before dinner, to work up an appetite. The sun had just gone down and the water was warm and inviting. But strangely enough, the pool was empty. I'd have thought that the pool would be brimming with swimmers; nothing like a dip in the pool to ease away the day's tensions at work, right?

As I was heading towards the pool, one of my neighbours looked incredulously at me and asked: "Going to swim? Alone?" It made me nervous.

As I was doing my laps, I heard thunder. It looked like it was going to rain. It was best, I thought, to finish up quickly.

Just then, I noticed a small child, a young boy, struggling in the deep end of the pool. How did he get there? I hadn't seen anyone. He looked like he was in trouble. He started to trash wildly about; the poor child was going to drown!

I swam towards him. But when I was about to reach him, he disappeared! Thinking that he might have submerged, I dived underwater. But there was no one there. I resurfaced, panting and looked around. There was no one else in the pool.

A chill ran down my spine. Whoever that child was, it wasn't human. I frantically swam to the edge of the pool and climbed up. I ran all the way up to my apartment, soaking wet, and, collapsed.

Later, my neighbours confirmed the pool was haunted.

Would you dare to take a plunge, Russell?

Russell Lee: That depends on what kind of swimming costume you wear!

SALT FOR SALE

Banana Loo Meow Chin, 12, student

After reading the story "Salt anyone?" in Book 9, my friend Judy, who's two years older than me, asked me if I was interested in making some easy money by selling salt to ghosts. I nodded my head and she told me to meet her at 10 o'clock that evening.

After having my dinner, I asked for my mum's permission to stay at Judy's house. She agreed and I went there. I looked at my watch. It was already 10.35 pm but Judy had not shown up yet.

After a while, I saw Judy with a big piece of white cloth and a few packets of salt. We took a taxi to the Choa Chu Kang cemetery.

When we reached there, it was nearly midnight. We quickly went to search for a tree. "Hey,

Banana! I found a good spot!" Judy said as she pointed to a tree. I turned my head and saw a big tree. We followed the instructions given. Soon, it was midnight.

Suddenly, a gentle wind blew. A pair of rotten outstretched hands came in front of us. Although we were terrified, we refused to look up. I poured some salt into the hands. The "ghost" dropped some money onto the white sheet. Then more and more hands stretched out.

At about four in the morning, the salt was sold out! Suddenly, an outstretched hand came up. We weren't prepared for this. Nothing in the book to cover this eventuality. We didn't move. Then the hands went away. After a while, a strong wind blew the white cloth away. I prayed hard for the day to break soon. After a while, I heard Judy whisper to me, "Banana, it's 7 am."

We quickly stood up and took the cloth and the money away. Like the story said, "Walk straight out and don't look back".

We split the money upon reaching home. After a few days, both of us ran a high fever. The doctors couldn't help.

My grandmother resorted to a bomoh. He mumbled some words that made us vomit. The bomoh said that we had made a spirit angry and that it wanted our lives. Luckily, my grandmother had consulted the bomoh early or we might have been dead by now!

Russell Lee: Stay away from the salt business. Anyway, too much of it will lead to high blood pressure.

"CENTURY"

Ruth Chua, 32, physiotherapist

Russell Lee, I know for a fact that ghosts can and do speak. Sometimes they speak through the person they possess although they are quite capable of speaking on their own. Many spirits in one person can also speak with one voice. How do I know this? From personal experience: this is my story.

I was the member of a cult group in 1978. It's leader spent much time in exorcising evil spirits. The group was based in Sembawang, next to the Sembawang Prison.

Initially, I was impressed for the man, "Brother John", seemed to win the battle against evil forces. But later I realised that the man was so evil that his group was a nesting place for every foul and evil spirit. And the leader himself was the main attraction.

In one incident, a possessed girl from Johor Baru was the subject of an exorcism.

"In the name of God, leave the girl!" Brother John commanded.

Joanna, the 27-year-old kindergarten teacher from Johor Baru, went into a fit.

"I know you!" it growled in a low voice. "I'll be coming for you!"

"Who are you?" John asked.

"Century, for there are 100 of us here!" This time it spoke in a female voice, sweet and gentle!

John was never able to exorcise the spirits.

He said later that it was because Joanna was wor-shipping the devil. I think that in that particular instance he was right. But in many other cases, the spirits were not exorcised because he didn't have the power to do so. In fact the spirits were mocking him, and using him to spread their influence!

When I realised this, I left the group. It wasn't an easy thing to do as I had been completely brainwashed by the cult.

John swore and cursed and shouted that I would burn forever in hell. I left anyway.

Now, even though it's been seven years since I left, the trauma and bitter memories of my entrapment in the cult comes flooding back whenever I'm reminded of the group or whenever I meet one of the cult's members.

Russell Lee: It's time for me to go but this last story is a healthy reminder of the reality of the spirit world. Ruth's experience is not uncommon and I intend to do an extensive piece on the damaging influence of cults in Book 11.

Don't be fooled: behind the cults are demonic forces that propel and energise them. Yes, spirits (both evil and good) are for real.

The ultimate aim of foul spirits that possess humans is to destroy both body and soul. They want as many people as possible to join them in Hell, their eventual destination.

Ghosts can also occupy the bodies of animals. Snakes and pigs are favourite targets. Animals are able to talk like humans when spirits enter them and use them. Strange but true. The story "Lady Whitesnake" in Book 9 is an example of how this can happen. In the Bible, there are accounts of snakes and donkeys talking.

It is also possible to communicate with spirits although this is an exercise that I would urge you to avoid.

And, there is a definite hierarchy in the spirit world. It is very similar to an army. There is the head honcho and his lieutenants, then the lower-ranking officers and warrant officers and multitudes of soldiers.

Spirits do actively influence the course of world events through their agents in the world. Don't be deceived — things aren't as simple as they seem. There is a titanic battle going on between the forces of good and evil. You ignore it at your own peril. I hope that these stories that I do in the True Singapore Ghost Stories series will help to give you some idea of this reality.

Ghosts are spirits — in other words they don't have any physical shape, contrary to what you may have been led to believe in the movies or books. They may take on a human or animal shape but that is only an outer covering which they can discard very easily.

My certainty of the above facts is the result of years and years of experience.

With that, goodbye and see you next time. In the meantime, write me if you have anything to say.

Sleep well.

The Angsana Russell Lee Writers' Contest (Book 10)

Win CASH and other prizes! Send in a story!

We are offering more than S$2,000/RM4,000 in cash and other mystery prizes. So send in your stories and letters.

The rules of the contest are simple. All you have to do is to write a ghost story, preferably based on a personal experience. You could also write on a general topic about ghosts. About 700 words will do; we are not fussy about length. We are fussy about entertainment value. Entries must be ORIGINAL, that is, they must be your own and unpublished. If your story is chosen for publication or if we think it's a good story, you win an amount up to S$200/RM400. The contest is open to all.

Winners will be announced in the next book but you must claim your prize within six months from the date of launch of the next book. We will write to winners but please make sure that you have listed your names and addresses clearly and correctly. Unclaimed prizes will be forfeited.

The entire copyright and all other rights to the published stories/letters will belong to Flame Of The Forest Publishing, the publishers.

We reserve the right to edit the stories to any extent.

When deciding the winners, age will be a consideration. The decisions of the publishers are final. Any interesting letter with photos and illustrations attached may also win prizes. We might publish the photos and illustrations as well. Send in as many entries as you like. Mail them to:

Russell Lee
Angsana Books
Flame Of The Forest Publishing Pte Ltd
Blk 5 Ang Mo Kio Industrial Park 2A
#07-22/23, AMK Tech II
Singapore 567760

OR Email your stories and letters to:
russelllee@flameoftheforest.com.

Don't forget to include the following: Name, Age, Gender, Address, Phone, Mobile, Email address, School and Occupation. If some details are not available, that's fine. If you could, please tell us which three stories you enjoyed most in this book.

We reserve the right to change the rules of the contest at any time if we think it is necessary.

Don't wait. Send us your story.

The Publishers
Flame Of The Forest Publishing Pte Ltd